# Unveiling Precognitive Dreams

## How Supporters and Opponents Bury the Truth

S.F. Heaven

# Unveiling Precognitive Dreams: How Supporters and Opponents Bury the Truth



**DISCLAIMER** This book explores themes related to precognitive dreams, psychology, and consciousness. It is based on the author's independent research and has yet to undergo widespread public or scientific validation.

**ISBN (Hardback):** 979-8-90329-167-0

**ISBN (Paperback):** 979-8-90329-169-4

**Published by:** Beijing Mengjing Jiemi Tech Center

*First Edition:  2026*

* * *

The core of science is acknowledging ignorance, and questioning keeps us humble while moving forward courageously.

* * *

# Table of Contents


PREFACE ........................................................................................... I

0.1 WHAT DOES "ALL DREAMS ARE PRECOGNITIVE" MEAN? ................... II

0.2 THE ORIGIN OF "ALL DREAMS ARE PRECOGNITIVE" ......................... IV

0.3 THE MISSION OF THIS BOOK ....................................................... VIII

0.4 HOW TO VERIFY THIS BOOK ............................................................ X

SECTION 1: OPPONENTS' OBJECTIONS TO PRECOGNITIVE

DREAMS ............................................................................................ 1

1.1 COINCIDENCE THEORY'S OBJECTIONS TO PRECOGNITIVE DREAMS ...................... 2

1.2 SUPERSTITION THEORY'S OBJECTIONS TO PRECOGNITIVE DREAMS ..................... 18

1.3 HALLUCINATION THEORY'S OBJECTIONS TO PRECOGNITIVE DREAMS ............... 34

1.4 TEMPORAL INDETERMINACY THEORY'S OBJECTIONS TO PRECOGNITIVE DREAMS

........................................................................................................ 41

1.5 PSYCHOLOGY'S OBJECTIONS TO PRECOGNITIVE DREAMS ................................... 48

SECTION 2: SUPPORTERS' MISCONCEPTIONS OF PRECOGNITIVE

DREAMS .......................................................................................... 59

2.1 POSTHUMOUS DREAM COMMUNICATION THEORY'S MISCONCEPTIONS OF

PRECOGNITIVE DREAMS ............................................................................. 59

2.2 ANTI-DREAM THEORY'S MISCONCEPTIONS OF PRECOGNITIVE DREAMS ............ 77

2.3 MISCONCEPTIONS ABOUT PRECOGNITIVE DREAMS IN DIVINATION ................... 87

2.4 MISCONCEPTIONS ABOUT PRECOGNITIVE DREAMS IN MYSTICAL THEORY ........ 99

SECTION 3: SUPPORTERS' MISREPRESENTATION OF "NON-PRECOGNITIVE DREAMS" .................................................................................... 113

3.1 WANG FU'S MISREPRESENTATION OF "NON-PROPHETIC DREAMS" .................... 114

3.2 JUNG'S MISREPRESENTATION OF "NON-PRECOGNITIVE DREAMS" .................... 122

3.3 CHRISTIANS' MISREPRESENTATION OF "NON-PRECOGNITIVE DREAMS" .......... 140

POSTSCRIPT ................................................................................................ 157

I. THE ORIGIN AND DEVELOPMENT OF THIS SERIES AND THIS BOOK .................... 157

II. INTRODUCTION TO THE FIRST THREE VOLUMES OF UNVEILING PRECOGNITIVE DREAMS ................................................................................................ 159

III. INTRODUCTION TO "UNVEILING PRECOGNITIVE DREAMS" VOLUME 5 ............ 162

IV. ABOUT THE AUTHOR ........................................................................... 165

V. OTHER ISSUES ................................................................................... 167

ii

# Preface

*Unveiling Precognitive Dreams* is a series consisting of 10 to 12 volumes, and this book, *How Supporters and Opponents Bury the Truth,* is the fourth volume. This entire series of books aims to prove a counterintuitive hypothesis that humanity has never considered: "All dreams are precognitive!"

Indeed, this appears absurd and utterly impossible, but please understand: precisely because it is absurd and impossible, the author posited this hypothesis and treated it with an extremely rigorous attitude! Only after years of exploration and verification, and once the chain of evidence was complete, did the author decide to write it as a series of works and present it to the public. If you doubt this, ask yourself: if this book lacked a solid core, what would the author rely on to sustain his lengthy argumentation of this hypothesis? If the author were purely indulging in fantasy, on what basis would he attract readers to maintain long-term interest in this book? This is not just one or two volumes, but more than ten! Nor is it calculated by the day, but by the year!

Just like a movie, without audience approval, how can there be a sequel? For a series of books, without genuine insight, how can there be subsequent installments? Since the author has progressed this far and dares to provide multiple paths of verification, it indicates that he must have already turned the impossible into the possible! Therefore, please rest assured; if you are someone interested in dreams or precognitive dreams, this series of books will certainly not let you down!

## 0.1 What Does "All Dreams Are Precognitive" Mean?

Precognitive dreams are dreams where you see something before it actually happens. Precognition means knowing something in advance. All dreams are precognitive, meaning all dreams can predict the future, and all people's dreams have foresight. Not a single dream is an exception to this. However, this precognition is limited to what a person's dream can foresee; it is from the dream's perspective, not the person's. Only if one could stand from the dream's perspective would it imply that the person can also foresee, but it is very difficult for a person to adopt the dream's perspective. Sometimes, people can also achieve precognition in a waking state, but this type of precognition is worlds apart from that in dreams. Waking-state precognition is based on experience and logic, whereas precognition in dreams directly enters the future and is a form of "superpower." If there were any human theory that could explain this phenomenon, the three physics theories of "time reversal," "four-dimensional space," and "quantum entanglement" might serve as a makeshift explanation.

How do precognitive dreams predict the future? It should be

obvious without saying: of course, most do so through "symbolism." Otherwise, if what you dream is what it is, then dreaming you caught a fish would mean you caught a fish in reality, but you might never go fishing; dreaming a deceased person is still alive would mean they are still alive in reality, which is clearly impossible. Therefore, anyone who assumes that a dream depicts exactly what will happen is being overly naive. In reality, precognitive dreams are typically expressed symbolically—not literally. This is a fundamental principle of dream interpretation.

As for how to express this in symbolic form? Take the simplest example: dreaming of "catching a fish": this kind of dream symbolizes gaining benefits, meaning that once someone has such a dream, it signifies that this person will gain something in some aspect of reality. Its correspondence with reality is: fish corresponds to benefits; catching corresponds to gaining, and the entire phrase "catching a fish" corresponds to "having gained benefits." Most dreams are constructed this way and are closely related to the future; it's just that some are simple, while others are complex.

The complex ones are not incomprehensible either, such as the idiom "meng bi sheng hua"—the Tang Dynasty romantic poet Li Bai dreamt of a flower blooming from the tip of his brush. Could it be that a flower truly grew from the tip of Li Bai's brush? No one interprets it this way, because everyone knows that it merely describes Li Bai's literary agility, how beautiful verses could be born from his pen, not that actual flowers grew. Clearly, this dream is another level of difficulty compared to the previous one, but it can likewise be deciphered by intelligent humans.

Even more complex is the dream of a "headless dragon" recorded in the *History of Song* (see Section 3), which everyone misunderstood at the time, but was later corrected. This shows that as long as anyone is willing to make the effort and recognize that understanding their own dreams is not a fantasy, then the possibility that the secrets of dreams will one day be uncovered by humanity becomes real. The mission of this book series is dedicated to precisely this. It no longer focuses solely on individual or a small number of precognitive dreams, but turns its gaze to all dreams, asserting that even those which are not precognitive dreams are, in fact, precognitive dreams. This thesis is undoubtedly more difficult and seemingly impossible. If it can be achieved, it will surely be a great boon to human society and become a true "watershed" in human history—before this, it could be called "Before Dreams," rather than "Anno Domini"! That is: using dreams to demarcate human history. Of course, this refers only to the great significance of this discovery, not that it must be so.

## 0.2 The Origin of "All Dreams Are Precognitive"

As is well known, humanity holds two diametrically opposed

views on precognitive dreams: one is the supportive view—acknowledging that only a small portion of dreams are precognitive, while most are not; the other is the opposing view—believing that no dream is precognitive, completely denying the former. Who is right and who is wrong? If the supporters are correct, how should the opponents' view be explained? After all, it is endorsed by modern science. If the opponents are correct, how can one persuade the supporters? Those are their personal experiences. For a long time, human understanding of precognitive dreams has been in a stalemate between the two sides, with neither able to convince the other. This, of course, is also the dilemma the author faces: on one hand, the author firmly believes in the existence of precognitive dreams and stands unswervingly on the side of supporters; on the other hand, the author is unable to convince the opponents. How can this deadlock be broken? One conceivable answer is: is it possible that even the supporters are incorrect, and there exists another possibility? That is, "all dreams or most dreams are precognitive," rather than "only a small minority!"

At first glance, this view seems even less credible because it contradicts common sense; however, common sense is not necessarily correct, and such examples are not uncommon. "The sun revolves around the earth" is a classic example, when in reality the opposite is true; the 2025 Nobel Prize in Physics is similar: the quantum tunneling effect, once thought to belong exclusively to the microscopic world, can also be observed in macroscopic circuits, demonstrating that so-called common sense is not truly common sense—as long as there are traces within common sense that defy common sense, the original common sense may be overturned and replaced by new common sense. And do precognitive dreams not fit this characteristic? On one hand, many people in life indeed have such experiences, yet our "common sense" tells people that they are false; on the other hand, humans do have cognitive limitations, so it is difficult to guarantee that past views are free from error. Given this, the possibility that precognitive dreams truly exist cannot be ruled out; it is simply that no one has found a way to prove it. Then, the next challenge is: how to capture this possibility and provide strong proof? The answer is the "hypothetical method"! Historical experience tells us that the hypothetical method is precisely the key to unlocking such dilemmas. The Nobel Prize in Physiology or Medicine in 1960, 1965, and 2005, as well as the Nobel Prize in Chemistry in 2005— these breakthroughs later recorded in history all originated from a hypothesis that ran counter to the consensus of the time. It was the "hypothetical method" that led scientists step by step closer to the truth. For precognitive dreams, why can we not make the same assumption? This is exactly the origin of the central thesis of this book—"all dreams are precognitive"—which likewise originates from a hypothesis.

You might ask: Why assume "all dreams" rather than "most dreams"? This is determined by logical thoroughness: only by assuming "all dreams" can one fundamentally prevent opponents from counterattacking; otherwise, you will forever be entangled with them, because they can always refute you with "Why are some dreams not precognitive dreams?" and then defeat you with seemingly scientific theories such as "coincidence, hallucination, wish fulfillment, sleep paralysis." Therefore, the reason for making such an assumption goes without saying. Clearly, only in this way can you leave them no loophole, fundamentally cut off their retreat, and make them completely give up; otherwise, they will always find a way to use their discourse power to besiege you, making it impossible for you to defend yourself.

The above is the origin of "all dreams are precognitive." It is both the hypothesis and the central thesis of this book, as well as the hypothesis and central thesis of this book series, *Unveiling Precognitive Dreams*. Science is about making bold assumptions, carefully verifying them, and then by presenting facts and reasoning, deducing that the hypothesis is not a hypothesis but a fact. Undoubtedly, this series has proven this hypothesis; otherwise, this book would not exist.

## 0.3 The Mission of This Book

No one would deny: if the near-impossible hypothesis that "all dreams are precognitive" could be confirmed, what enormous waves it would stir! However, despite the immense impact, providing a thorough proof of it is a difficult problem, which is one of the reasons why this series of books needs to be unfolded across multiple volumes. For what you face is a "tangled mess": it requires layer-by-layer peeling, step-by-step piecing together, and long-term advancement—there is neither transparency nor a ready-made path. Just like the blind men feeling an elephant, each person can only perceive a part through touch, and to know what kind of elephant it is, one must piece together every fragment felt by everyone; but for the blind, how easy is that? And in the face of dreams, is not man precisely that blind man? It is precisely for this reason that humanity is deeply mired in two types of misconceptions regarding precognitive dreams: On one hand, opponents habitually label precognitive dreams with pseudoscientific tags such as "hallucinations, coincidences, wish fulfillment, sleep paralysis," regarding them as superstition; on the other hand, proponents are keen to describe precognitive dreams as so-called "scientifically inexplicable" mysterious narratives such as "posthumous dream communication, past lives, ghost pressing down, mysticism," viewing superstition as reasonable—while the two sides appear to be diametrically opposed, they are unknowingly burying the truth together. The following eleven questions are part of the many instances of this "double burial" accumulated over a long period in human society; this book's revelation of each question is a subversion and reconstruction of existing human cognition, and this is precisely the clearest embryonic form of that "elephant" to date:

(1) Why is it equally untenable for opponents to regard precognitive dreams as coincidence?

(2) Why is it incorrect for opponents to explain the common sensation of déjà vu as a hallucination?

(3) Why is it both correct and incorrect for opponents to view belief in precognitive dreams as superstition?

(4) Opponents view precognitive dreams as being realized through infinite postponement; why is this rooted in ignorance?

(5) Why is psychology's opposition to precognitive dreams more absurd than believing in precognitive dreams themselves?

(6) Why does interpreting "nightmare disorder" as "sleep paralysis" or "ghost pressing down" cause greater truths to be obscured?

(7) Since the phenomenon of "the deceased appearing in dreams" is also a form of precognitive dream, why is the understanding of "Posthumous dream communication" by its proponents considered superstition?

(8) Why is it wrong for proponents to claim that precognitive

dreams are reversed?

(9) Why do Christians who believe in precognitive dreams misinterpret the Bible's teachings on dream interpretation?

(10) Why are precognitive dreams a science rather than mysticism?

Truth and fallacy cannot coexist; once a fallacy is exposed, the truth becomes evident. In the realm of cognition, the removal of error itself means making room for truth—when old perceptions collapse, a new paradigm can be established. This is the mission of this book, *Unveiling Precognitive Dreams: How Supporters and Opponents Bury the Truth*; it was born to expose these errors and clear away these fallacies.

## 0.4 How to Verify This Book

Verifying this book is very simple. Next, I will design three approaches, all of which can guide you through the verification process, making it traceable; of course, you can also create your own method, but regardless of the path taken, the result should be definitive, not ambiguous. If there is uncertainty, ruling out your own reasons is sufficient to falsify this book.

First, start with the dream examples in this book, following the principle of "drawing a gourd from a template." This book provides a large number of dream examples, including dreams of the deceased, dreams of murder, dreams of funerals, dreams of disasters, dreams of sleep paralysis, dreams of interpersonal conflicts, dreams of work, dreams of repairing objects, and so on. The explanations are very definite, one is one, and two is two, so definite that you might find them too simple. As long as your dream is related to these examples, you will inevitably come to a similar conclusion as the book. If you can't, excluding your own reasons, then the book is wrong.

Second, start with logic. Dreams are as numerous as grains of sand in the desert, and no one can prove every single dream, just as you cannot verify that every grain of sand is indeed sand. However, logically speaking, if you can prove that one grain of sand is indeed sand, then all the remaining grains of sand must also be sand, because this can be determined logically. Dreams are the same. If you can prove that one dream is equivalent to proving a thousand or ten thousand dreams, or able to prove that all dreams of a certain kind are precognitive dreams, then you can logically prove it. As long as you can ensure that the logic is correct, there is no need to prove every single dream. However, you must understand that even if we can logically prove that "all dreams are precognitive," it does not mean that we can decipher all dreams. The reason is simple: after all dreams are not like sand that always stays there. Dreams are abstract and gradually forgotten over time, which makes it very difficult for us to decode all dreams.

For someone who hasn't attended university, would they be able to solve university exam questions? Of course not. But does that mean those exam questions have no answers? And for someone who has attended university, can they solve all university exam questions? Certainly not. Does that mean the unsolved questions have no answers? Of course not. The same logic applies to proving whether all dreams are precognitive. You can't claim a dream isn't precognitive just because you don't understand it, as long as we ensure the logic used to prove "all dreams are precognitive" is correct, there is no need to insist that every dream must be deciphered.

However, following the dream interpretation path outlined in this book, after a period of learning, cracking more than 80% of dreams should be easy! As for the progress, it depends on whether you dream often and whether you are willing to work hard to decipher these dreams. If you are a very diligent person, cracking half of your dreams within six months and reaching 80% within a year should be achievable. I am currently at 90% or more, close to 100%. Most people will eventually fall into the 90%-100% range. Because the rules are constant, only your effort changes. As long as you are willing to work hard, you will inevitably reach this range, just like a car driver. As long as you drive often, you will eventually become an experienced driver, even if you have not undergone formal training.

Third, start with the questions in your heart. I believe everyone will have countless questions when reading this book, and these questions must be answered within its pages. If they can be found, it proves the book is correct. So, what are people's doubts about this book? Naturally, there are many. Here are just nine examples:

(1) If "all dreams are precognitive" is true, such a big secret would inevitably have some clues exposed right under human eyes. The question is, are there such clues?

(2) If "all dreams are precognitive" is true, there must be definite indicators that can be observed by humans, just like the indicators that the Earth is round. So, do dreams have such indicators? (Indicators are clearer evidence than signs; if signs are still somewhat vague, indicators are more certain.)

(3) If "all dreams are precognitive" is true, then among the precognitive dreams already discovered, there must necessarily exist some invariant, universal fundamental law that can be observed by humans. Does such a law exist?

(4) If "all dreams are precognitive" is true, there must be a kind of logic that can subject it to intellectual scrutiny. Dreams are like rivers, flowing every day, with the old going and the new coming. If there is no such logic that can encompass this situation, then any related proof is meaningless. What kind of logic can achieve this?

(5) If "all dreams are precognitive" is true, then there must be a way to prove it in a laboratory through scientific experiments. The

fact is that scientists have conducted countless experiments and have not been able to prove it. Since scientific experiments cannot prove it, how can you prove it?

(6) If "all dreams are precognitive" is true, then the phenomenon of "ghost pressing down" in dreams must also be precognitive dreams. However, medical science indicates that this is merely a manifestation of "sleep paralysis" during sleep. How would you explain this?

(7) If "all dreams are precognitive" is true, there must be direct evidence to demonstrate this. Where is this direct evidence?

(8) If "all dreams are precognitive" is true, and assuming you are correct, how do you know that other people's dreams are as well? Can others repeat your method?

(9) If "all dreams are precognitive" is true, are you confident that you could design an experiment to reveal the truth publicly within a few days?

The above are just a few examples, and there are many other questions not listed. For instance, whenever one dreams of a "deceased person," traditional Chinese belief holds that paper money should be burned, saying they lack money or need "deliverance." Could this also be a precognitive dream? Such questions are countless for everyone and seem difficult to answer, but in fact, they are not. The reason you find it difficult is because "all beginnings are hard"; the first step is not easy to take. Once you take that step and taste the sweetness, everything becomes smooth sailing. Wherein:

The answers to items 1 and 3 are in the first volume.

The answer to item 2 is in the third volume.

The answer to item 4 is in the first three volumes.

The answer to item 5 is in the second volume.

The answer to item six is revealed in Book Five.

The answer to item seven is present from Book Six through to the final book.

The answer to item eight is in Book Eleven.

As for the answer to item nine, wait until you've finished the entire series — by then such an experiment no longer needs my design; anyone could devise it.

The answer to The Dream of the Dead is in volumes five and six: volume five explains the reasoning, and volume six provides the evidence and conclusions. These dreams are also an important source of confidence for me. If you can prove the errors in this book based on such dreams, it would be tantamount to negating the "foundation" of this book and destroying the author's confidence! If you wish to refute the author, you might as well start with these dreams.

The proof process in this book is, in fact, a demonstration and an explanation, If you are willing to put in the effort, following the methods in this book will surely lead you to the same conclusions as the author. Therefore, this book is actually a demonstration book as well as an instruction manual. This book offers countless pieces of evidence for your reference, including corroborative, circumstantial, and direct evidence. No matter what kind of evidence, it is abundantly present throughout this book. Regarding this, I dare to guarantee:

If you can find that the direct evidence in this book is wrong, excluding your own reasons, then you do not need to read a single word of this book anymore, just directly dismiss this book!

If you can find that the supporting evidence or circumstantial evidence in this book contradicts the direct evidence or conclusion of this book, excluding your own reasons, then you do not need to read a single word of this book anymore, just directly dismiss this book!

Whether it is corroborating, circumstantial, or direct evidence, this book is "one is one, two is two", without the slightest ambiguity. Anyone can use this to determine whether their own dream is the same too, very easy to distinguish. So tell me, can this book be verified and replicated by a third party?

Moreover, I am willing to accept anyone's challenge, but I'm afraid I might be overwhelmed. If that's the case, then everyone can choose a representative! Actually, there's no need for a challenge, because the author's conclusion is very simple. Take the "ghost pressing down" discussed from the fourth and fifth volumes, and the "dreams of the deceased" discussed in the fifth and sixth volumes, for example; their conclusions are as simple as $1+1=2$, understandable to everyone. What kind of relationship do they have with the future? To give an analogy, it's like you're looking for something in a dimly lit room, and this item emits its own light, making it very easy to find. And it's not just these two types of dreams; all other types of dreams are the same. The biggest difficulty in science lies in breakthroughs; once a breakthrough is made, it's smooth sailing. Given this, what are you challenging? You only need to challenge yourself. As long as there is determination, there is no fortress that cannot be conquered!

# Section 1: Opponents' Objections to Precognitive Dreams

Opponents' objections to precognitive dreams refer to the negative views regarding the authenticity, rationality, and validity of precognitive dreams put forward by those who oppose them. These opinions mainly include the coincidence theory, superstition theory, hallucination theory, and temporal indeterminacy theory, and are shackles imposed on precognitive dreams by opponents based on their own misunderstandings.

Skepticism itself is a good thing, but not all skepticism is constructive; some of it is destructive. The key lies in the manner of skepticism: destructive skepticism only questions others, not oneself; while healthy skepticism treats everyone equally, including oneself. In reality, most people fall into the first category—even if they occasionally self-reflect, it's merely a formality to reinforce their own biases. In fact, if anyone raising objections to precognitive dreams could uphold the principle of "fairness," deeply reflecting on their own limitations while objecting to others, it would not be difficult to discover that those opposing voices are equally unreliable, and thus proceed with caution.

## 1.1 Coincidence Theory's Objections to Precognitive Dreams

Coincidence refers to an accidental agreement or an exact match, the opposite of "deliberate." It speaks to chance rather than inevitability. The coincidence theory is one of the most heard arguments among those who question precognitive dreams, suggesting that such dreams are merely coincidences—random occurrences with no absolute significance, mere probabilistic events. Below are the three most frequently cited examples:

(1) There are many, many people on this planet, over 8 billion. When the sample is large enough, anything incredible can happen. Moreover, everyone dreams, and the number of things they dream about is astronomical. How could coincidences not occur?

(2) If someone dreams of a plane crash, and a plane happens to crash, the dream will be considered prophetic. If it's not a plane, but a train or even a car accident, it's very likely that the dream will also be considered prophetic. Therefore, the same dream can actually correspond to many facts, and the rationalization psychological effect of people will connect the dream with these facts, and then define it as a dream prophecy.

(3) A dream being exactly the same as something in the future is simply a matter of probability. It's like when you're in a good mood one day and DIY a piece of clothing, only to go out and find someone wearing the exact same outfit - it's just probability.

Such arguments may seem plausible at first glance. As a minority within the realm of dreams, viewing precognitive dreams as mere probability or coincidence is not unreasonable. Yet people overlook a crucial question: does this probability reflect the inherent nature of precognitive dreams—since most dreams are indeed not precognitive—or is it simply that dreams are too complex for humans to grasp, allowing us to discover them only occasionally? If the latter is true, it doesn't disprove precognitive dreams. After all, dreams exist beyond the normal scope of human understanding, so occasional discoveries are natural. If the issue lies with dreams themselves—that most dreams are indeed not precognitive—then the coincidence explanation holds water. Clearly, opponents fail to grasp this distinction, never considering that they themselves might be the ones making the mistake.

The recklessness and confidence of coincidence theorists resemble an ancient allegory recorded in Volume 6, Part 2 of the "Collected Commentaries on Zhuangzi," in the chapter "Autumn Floods" of the Outer Chapters, which states, "The frog in the well knows nothing of the sea, the summer insect knows nothing of ice, and the narrow scholar knows nothing of the Dao."

It means: You cannot speak of the sea to a frog in a well—it is confined by its narrow abode. You cannot speak of ice to a summer insect—it is bound by its season. You cannot speak of the Dao to a narrow scholar—he is shackled by his doctrines. Now that you have emerged from the riverbanks and beheld the vast sea, you realize your own insignificance, and thus you may be spoken to of the great principles.

Aren't humans equally prone to such errors when it comes to the matter of precognitive dreams? A person with limited knowledge, lack of experience, and stubborn self-righteousness, who fails to engage in self-reflection, will inevitably stray far from the point and mislead others.

### 1.1.1 The Flaws of the Coincidence Theory

If something is not true, it will inevitably have many flaws exposed to the public, and this book is no exception. If this book is not the truth, there must be many flaws that you can find; if you cannot find any, it means the book is most likely correct. The coincidence theory is the same; if the coincidence theory is wrong, there must be many flaws. The example I give below is like this. In this example, the female nurse opposes the coincidence theory and insists that precognitive dreams do exist because she found flaws in the coincidence theory. Even though there is evidence showing that precognitive dreams are an objective reality, people still firmly deny it, as if encountering "well frogs," "summer insects," and "narrow-minded scholars." To make them change, they must be the discoverers themselves.

She said, "Don't tell me that precognitive dreams are just coincidences anymore. There are too many such coincidences, and

I'm not making this up. Let me start with the most recent discovery. I'll briefly describe the dream content. One night I dreamed of a man in a suit and tie who was controlling me in every way, which made me very annoyed and suppressed. The next night, I dreamed of the Republican era, where the second son of the Gao family wanted to marry me."

"Now I'm interning at my workplace (a hospital), and a senior colleague is responsible for supervising me. His surname is Gao, he's from a wealthy family, and he's the second son in his family. Plus, he always wears dress pants and leather shoes. However, he's actually a year younger than me, only 20 years old. It's rare for someone to dress like this every day, and he really does control me in every way, just like I felt in the dream."

"Back in March or April, I knew I would be starting my internship in August, but I had no idea where I would be going or what people I would meet, and I had never even been to that hospital." (Note: The time she posted this was late August.)

"If it were a coincidence, then there are too many things that match up perfectly. For example, first, he indeed has the surname Gao, just like in my dream. Second, he is indeed the second son in his family. Third, he's only 20 years old, and while his work environment doesn't require formal attire, he still wears dress pants and leather shoes. Fourth, he has been controlling me in every way since my internship began, giving me the same oppressive feeling as in the dream. So I personally don't think it's a coincidence, especially since I've had precognitive dreams before."

"My previous precognitive dream was about seeing a woman giving a speech by the podium after the college entrance exam. Later, when university started, during the class cadre election, a girl indeed acted differently from others. She said she wanted to lighten the atmosphere, so instead of standing in the center of the podium, she spoke from the side. Eventually, I ended up having a very bad relationship with her."

"Another time, I had arranged with classmates to visit an unfamiliar city the next day. The night before, I dreamed I was floating in a place covered entirely in green construction netting - the kind used on buildings. The next day, when we went to that city we'd never visited before, the downtown area was under construction with roads and buildings being repaired. While no other parts of the city were under construction, the exact route we had planned to explore was completely covered in green construction netting."

"Yet another precognitive dream involved me injuring my foot. Not long after, my foot did indeed get injured, and it was quite serious."

"One more dream from the past. During my university years, I didn't go home often, so I rarely had the chance to visit my grandmother in my hometown. During this period, my grandmother became ill, but my parents didn't tell me because they were worried I would be concerned. I dreamed that I went to my grandmother's house, but the entrance was different from reality - there were several large black dogs staring at me, and I was terrified. I can't clearly remember the dreams from those few days, but I was very worried about my grandmother in the dreams. Later, when I returned home for the holidays, my grandmother had lost so much weight she was unrecognizable. She had developed a stomach illness. A few days prior, she had gone to Beijing for examinations to determine what was wrong, and her tumor markers were more than five times the normal level. As a medical student, I knew for certain that there was something growing in my grandmother's stomach." (Note: Later, Grandma was finally diagnosed with stomach cancer and passed away a few months after this post.[1])

The above are the dreams she has had, these dreams belong to the "dreams that have been fulfilled many times in a row between different dreams" mentioned earlier, such dreams often have an impact on a person, which makes her firmly believe in the existence of precognitive dreams, of course, not all places can make her understand, so she posted to ask. She said: "My current confusion is that in the dream, he wants to marry me, but I refuse because I've never met him. In reality, we both can't stand each other." At this point, I understood why she was asking. To help her express

---

[1] https://tieba.baidu.com/p/4755478513

herself more clearly, I asked her to provide more details. The following is the dream of what she wanted to ask after the addition:

First dream: A man whose face I couldn't see, dressed in a suit. At first, he trusted no one, but then I did something—I don't know what—that made him completely trust me. After that, whatever I did, he would consider it for me and control me, which made me feel very oppressed. The whole process of this dream seemed like a psychological feeling.

The second dream: In the Republic of China era, the second son of the Gao family wanted to marry me, but I had never even seen him, and I didn't know whether I should agree. Later, I saw a mother on the street taking her two daughters to the Gao family for a matchmaking meeting, pushing a bicycle. The younger one was only about five or six years old, sitting on the bike, and the older one was about 12, walking beside it. I thought to myself, since this mother is so eager to go to the matchmaking meeting, maybe the second son of the Gao family isn't bad after all. Perhaps I should agree to this marriage.

How should these two dreams be interpreted? The first dream is actually a direct reflection of her personal experience during her internship. Internships always require following the arrangements of senior colleagues, and as a student, she inevitably felt a bit uncomfortable. This dream is a reflection of that reality. The second dream is a bit more complex, but it is not difficult to understand if a few key points are clarified.

First is the meaning of "marry."

Second is what the mother and her two children respectively symbolize.

Considering her actual situation, "marry" obviously refers to cooperation at work, and successful cooperation means the success of the "marriage." In this way, the reason why the dream ends with "I might as well agree to this marriage" can be understood: it is because she ultimately overcame her resistance to her senior and was able to cooperate with him freely and without restraint; The mother seen on the street is likely referring to her teacher, and the two daughters the mother is with probably represent classmates who are interning with her. Since they are students, they need to grow, so children appear in the dream; and because they also need to cooperate with their senior at work, a matchmaking scenario similar to hers appears in the dream. So, besides the above meanings, will she and her senior colleague develop a marital relationship during her internship? This is also what the dreamer is concerned about, and the answer is no. The dream also provides an answer to this point, because the person who will marry her is from the Republican era, not in the same time and space, so of course it won't happen. At this point, it becomes clear why this nurse deeply believes in precognitive dreams, because she has experienced many such dreams, experiencing "multiple consecutive verifications between different dreams."

To simultaneously dream of the other person's surname, their birth order in the family, their clothing, and their psychological feelings cannot be explained by coincidences other than precognitive dreams. Moreover, similar dreams have occurred multiple times. When precognitive dreams happen repeatedly to one person, chance becomes inevitable. Therefore, there is a reason why those who believe in precognitive dreams do so: they have experienced them, especially repeatedly. When such experiences occur time and again, the theory of mere coincidence becomes difficult to believe. What does this suggest? It suggests that the coincidence theory has its flaws, and as such, it remains possible for it to be overturned!

## 1.1.2 Comparison of Two Coincidences

In fact, speaking only of "coincidence," as long as you are willing to compare the "coincidences" of precognitive dreams with coincidences in daily life, it is not difficult to discover that there is a world of difference between the two. Even if you have never experienced a precognitive dream, you can still do so using other people's cases.

The first case below is a coincidence that I found online, and it is also a common coincidence in life. This coincidence was once rated as the number one coincidence event in the world by a magazine in Washington, USA; the second case is the so-called "coincidence" of a precognitive dream, which almost exactly predicted the predicament hurdler Liu Xiang encountered during the London Olympics. Because people had high expectations for Liu Xiang's event, this incident caused quite a stir, and the dream was reported by many media outlets. Similar "coincidences" are hard to convincingly explain as mere coincidences anymore, but unfortunately, no one has taken it seriously.

(1) A common coincidence in life: An American single woman, Williamde, once forgot to bring her keys when she went out. Just as she was at a loss outside her home, the mailman delivered a letter from her brother, and inside the envelope was exactly a key to her house! In the letter, her brother mentioned that when he visited last time, Williamde had given him a key to the front door, and it wasn't until he returned to Washington that he realized he had forgotten to return it, so he had to mail it back to her.

(2) The "Coincidence" of Precognitive Dreams: On August 7, 2012, at 11:11 AM, a netizen named "Backpacking Traveler" posted a Weibo message: "Last night I had a dream that Liu Xiang was injured, tripping over the first hurdle. Then, to avoid being scolded like in 2008, he limped to the finish line." He posted this dream online purely out of curiosity, but he never expected it to come true just six hours later! At around 5 PM, during the preliminary round of the 110-meter hurdles at the London Olympics, Liu Xiang, the hurdler, fell at the first hurdle, just as the

netizen had dreamed, and hopped to the finish line on one foot!

At first glance, the above two coincidences may not seem to be much different, but if you are willing to study them carefully, you will still find that there are actually very different things, which can be summarized into six points:

First, the difficulty of coincidence is different. If we use probability to calculate whether the "coincidence" of a precognitive dream or a common coincidence in life is more difficult, we will find that the "coincidence" of a precognitive dream is far more difficult than a common coincidence in life. Those interested may wish to calculate the probability of having a precognitive dream like "The Traveler with a Backpack." This value should include: the probability of dreaming of Liu Xiang; the probability of dreaming of Liu Xiang falling in a race; the probability of dreaming of Liu Xiang falling at the first of a total of ten hurdles to be crossed; the probability that Liu Xiang, after falling, would worry about having to withdraw from the race midway due to a leg injury like in the 2008 Olympics and being scolded, and thus having to continue jumping to the finish line; and the probability of dreaming of the entire process described above. As for coincidences in life, the probability of a brother finding a key that hasn't been returned and then mailing it to his sister is as high as 50%; the probability is smaller only if the sister forgets to bring her key and the brother happens to mail the key. At this point, it is clear which coincidence has a smaller probability. Obviously, the probability of the precognitive dream made by "The Traveler with a Backpack" is much smaller than the probability of sending the key. The smaller the probability, the greater the difficulty.

Second, the dimension of coincidence is different. Coincidences in life, meeting someone, just meeting; The birthday is the same, just the birthday; a plane crash, just a plane crash; In the previous example of "forgetting to bring keys", forgetting to bring the key, just happening to be sent by someone, is a point-to-point one-time coincidence, like the crossing of two rays, just crossed once, very simple, completely belonging to low latitudes. The "coincidences" in precognitive dreams are mostly high-dimensional, multi-layered, and even dynamic "coincidences." Even with constant changes and movement, they can still "coincide," with every gesture and action aligning perfectly. In this example, the dreamer not only dreamed of Liu Xiang falling, but also dreamed about which hurdle he fell at, whether he withdrew or continued the race, and why Liu Xiang hopped on one foot to the finish line. The timing of the dream was also just right—it was dreamed that day and happened that afternoon. Not only was the outcome exactly the same, but the timing, process, and reasons also basically matched. Can you say this kind of "coincidence" is the same as coincidences in everyday life? This is not an isolated case, wasn't it the same for the female nurse mentioned above who dreamed that the second son of the Gao family wanted to marry her? The other person's surname, their birth order in the family, their clothing, and the psychological feelings all matched perfectly; As for the author of this book, isn't the second recorded dream also a similar manifestation? At that time, a tenant's mother came to visit her son, and her profession and attire were exactly the same as in the author's dream. Can you call this a coincidence? Unless the author dreams of that tenant's mother every day!

Third, the subject of coincidence is different. Coincidences in life occur between different subjects. In this example, one forgets their keys while another delivers them—this describes a coincidence between two distinct subjects; whereas the "coincidence" in precognitive dreams involves two objects belonging to the same subject. Dreaming of Liu Xiang falling, only for Liu Xiang to actually fall, appears to occur between two subjects. Yet in reality, Liu Xiang merely appears passively within the dreamer's vision. Liu Xiang remains unaware that anyone would dream of him, and no direct connection exists between them. Thus, this constitutes a "coincidence" inherent to the same event itself. This kind of "coincidence" is more like an overlap, as if one is a shadow and the other a solid entity, clearly different from coincidences in life; it is an attribute of oneself, with the self as the subject.

Fourth, the host of the coincidence is different. The

"coincidence" of precognitive dreams is always related to a person's brain, which is a "coincidence" between the dream made by the brain and what happens, just as the brain is their host. As far as the "backpack traveler" is concerned, we can completely regard his dream as being related only to his own brain, that is: the "backpack traveler" dreamed of tomorrow's events, and tomorrow's events were presented in his brain, which was his own affairs, as if the brain was the host of this "coincidence", or this "coincidence" needed a host like this, and the coincidence in life passed away, like a shooting star in the sky, fleeting without leaving a trace, and it didn't matter whether a host was needed or not.

Fifth, the number of coincidences is different. arable events, the "coincidences" in precognitive dreams always outnumber those in real life because precognitive dreams have an extra "dream" aspect of "coincidence." Take the example of "an older brother giving his younger sister a key." If this were a precognitive dream, the number of "coincidences" would be: forgetting the key in the dream and then dreaming of someone delivering the key, that's one; forgetting the key in reality and then someone actually delivering the key in reality, that's another one, totaling two. However, forgetting the key in reality and someone delivering the key is only one coincidence in real life. Thus, under the same conditions, the "coincidences" in precognitive dreams will always be at least one more than the coincidences in real life, a point that people completely overlook.

Sixth, the reality of coincidences is different. Coincidences in everyday life generally already exist and are inferable and predictable. For example, the third example at the beginning of this article: "It's like when you're in a good mood one day and DIY a piece of clothing, only to go out and find someone wearing the exact same outfit - it's just probability." In that example, both the clothing and the person already exist; what will happen in the future can be completely predicted. But coincidences in precognitive dreams mostly concern things that did not exist in the past, and are hard to predict. Could you predict in which hurdle Liu Xiang would fall? You can only predict that he might fall, but not how he would fall. The key is that the timing of the dream just happens to match — you dream it and it happens, not that you repeatedly dream it and then it comes true once. It's like one time I dreamed that someone who could never possibly look for me came looking for me. If I often dreamed of that person coming for me and then one day that person happened to come, that would be a coincidence; but precognitive dreams are not like that. When it is destined that the person could never look for me, I could never have such a dream. Only when it is destined that the person will look for me can I dream of it, as if my dream was plainly born for that event.

Of course, you could also say that the examples of precognitive dreams cited in this article are rather special, but when you say this, it is actually only because you do not yet understand, since precognitive dreams are graded; the fact that these examples are special does not mean that other dreams are not precognitive dreams, it is just that they are of different grades. Regarding this point, I have already discussed it in the first volume; if you can thoroughly master it, you will understand.

You don't know until you compare, and once you do, the difference is staggering! This shows just how different the "coincidences" in precognitive dreams are from everyday coincidences. Therefore, dismissing precognitive dreams as mere "coincidences" feels more like a convenient excuse than the truth. This implies that while people have reasons to believe these dreams are coincidental, the outcome would likely be very different if they were willing to take the matter seriously. Take the student nurse mentioned above: although she understood many of her dreams, there were always problems she couldn't solve. When she turned to me for help in interpreting those vague dreamscapes, she discovered that even the most bizarre elements had significant connections to reality, and the ambiguities held hidden meanings. If one continues to explore in this manner, would those problems remain problems? Looking back then, would precognitive dreams still seem like such a small fraction of the whole? The result would certainly be vastly different! Why was the author's hypothesis proven successful? It is precisely because the results turned out this way; otherwise, success would have been impossible!

**Short-answer question:**

According to the division of fulfillment levels, indicate what level of fulfillment does the dream of "Traveler in a Backpack" belong? And list the corresponding fulfillment points.

## 1.2 Superstition Theory's Objections to Precognitive Dreams

Superstition theory is the second most commonly heard argument when humans question precognitive dreams. In daily life, whenever I talk to people about precognitive dreams, before I can even explain in detail, I am ridiculed as superstitious; those who have just experienced precognitive dreams, when sharing such experiences with others, first mock themselves as superstitious, saying that they are clearly atheists but still believe in these things, and then share their experiences; when I consulted a publisher about publishing this book, the publisher dismissed my explanations and directly said my book does not conform to science, shutting me out. Nowadays, there are already very few people who believe in precognitive dreams. The prevalence of superstition theory has further numbed those who might soon experience precognitive dreams, making them mistakenly believe that only denying precognitive dreams represents science. This is undoubtedly a huge obstacle to the discovery of precognitive dreams. So what makes people mistakenly believe that precognitive dreams are superstitions? And what criteria do they use to judge whether a person is superstitious? Without clarifying these issues, you can't possibly know right from wrong, and any doubt is irresponsible.

## 1.2.1 Why People Consider Precognitive Dreams to Be Superstition

Advocating for science and opposing superstition is certainly the right thing to do, but being right does not necessarily mean people can actually do what is right. If people fail to maintain a rigorous attitude toward certain issues, they may end up doing the opposite of what is right—either treating non-superstitious things as superstition, or treating superstitious things as non-superstitious. Today, prophetic dreams being regarded as superstition by us falls into the former category; certain superstitions in our traditional culture being viewed as normal falls into the latter category.

There are two definitions of superstition online: one refers to believing in non-existent things such as gods and ghosts; the other generally refers to blind faith and worship. That is, if someone believes that gods and ghosts exist, then this person is considered superstitious. In our traditional culture, the scriptures of Buddhism and Taoism, as well as temples and Taoist temples, are filled with various gods and ghosts. According to the definition, they are undoubtedly representatives of superstition. So what is the relationship between viewing gods and ghosts as superstition and precognitive dreams? Could it be that believing in precognitive dreams means believing in gods and ghosts? There is indeed a basis for this statement. In the scriptures of Buddhism and Taoism, there is indeed the idea that dreams are caused by "gods and ghosts." As stated in the Buddhist scripture *Abhidharma Mahavibhasa Shastra*: "Caused by others means that dreams occur due to the influence of deities, immortals, spirits, ghosts, incantations, medicinal herbs, thoughts of superiors, and guidance from sages and virtuous beings." Of course, this is just one of the many meanings explained by the Buddhist scriptures, but it is enough to show that they do hold this view. But the question is, why do people not say that believing in Buddhism and Taoism is superstition, but that believing in precognitive dreams is superstition? After the author's research, it turns out that there is a problem of unclear concept of "God".

Some of us may seem to be opposing "God," but in reality, they don't fully understand what "God" is, and they don't even know the differences between the gods in Buddhism and Taoism and those in Confucianism and Western religions. I have asked many people I encountered what "God" is and to define it. Their usual response is to be speechless, stuttering, and retreating, with no one truly able to answer. Many people's understanding of "God" is merely a matter of holding atheism as a sentiment, believing that as long as they adhere to atheism, they are correct and represent progress. Why did I ask them to define "God"? Because through their answers, I could understand how they conceptualize "God." If their understanding of "God" is that of the gods in Buddhism and Taoism, then their atheistic views are correct, as those are all "human-shaped gods." Humans cannot become gods. If humans could become gods, then Chairman Mao in the memorial hall would be our current China's biggest god. But where do you see this god of Chairman Mao? He never admitted that the Cultural Revolution was wrong, yet you say it was wrong. Why doesn't he come out to argue with you? Thus, treating humans as "gods" is a form of self-deception, not only deceiving others but also oneself.

Looking at the word "God" alone, it's just a symbol. If you limit yourself to this symbol without delving into its meaning, it means you haven't truly understood its essence. In that case, your so-called "atheistic" thought is bound to be a mess! The unclear concept of "God" cannot be entirely blamed on atheism. As history has progressed, even Confucian scholars today can't distinguish the differences between the Gods of Confucianism and those of Buddhism and Taoism. "Famous Confucian scholars who revered Confucius also worshiped Buddha; soldiers who believed in A today believe in D tomorrow." Why did Lu Xun say this? It's because although Confucianism has a clear definition of God, later Confucians had long deviated from Confucius and were assimilated by Buddhism and Taoism. Their God had already been replaced by the Gods of Buddhism and Taoism, and they began to worship Buddha. It's unimaginable for Confucianism to worship Buddha. After Buddhism entered China, many anti-Buddhist warriors emerged from Confucianism, famously including Fan Zhen in the Northern and Southern Dynasties, Han Yu, Li Ao, Du Mu, and Ouyang Xiu in the Tang Dynasty, Shi Jie, Zhang Zai, and Zhu Xi in the Song Dynasty, Wang Yangming in the Ming Dynasty, and Wang Fuzhi, Huang Zongxi, and Gu Yanwu in the late Ming and early Qing Dynasties. It wasn't until the Qing Dynasty, when emperors favored Buddhism, that the voices of Confucian anti-Buddhism gradually subsided. This means that after the Qing Dynasty, Buddhism and Taoism had completely established themselves in China, and Confucianism had to integrate with the two religions.

Although Buddhism and Taoism today are not as influential as in the past, they still hold significant appeal. The increasingly grand Buddha statues in our major scenic spots and the traditional funeral rites and various folk customs in our society reveal their deep emotional connection with our nation! Thus, even though our society appears to have transformed into one of atheists—where most people are not Buddhist disciples, lay devotees, or readers of Buddhist scriptures—subconsciously, we still maintain a fondness for these two religions, which have become ingrained in our traditional culture. Unconsciously, we are reluctant to dismiss them as mere superstition. It is precisely because of this chaotic situation that when Western atheism spread to our country, the gods in our atheism should have referred to the gods of Buddhism and Taoism, but they were inadvertently influenced by Western atheist trends and became their personified creator gods. This way, the "atheism" in our atheism no longer means "without" the gods of our Buddhism and Taoism, but rather "without" the personalized God of the West. And that "shapeless" God of Confucianism, which had long been eradicated by the combined efforts of Buddhism and Taoism, disappeared without a trace. So much so that the "god" in "Confucius did not speak of strange powers, rebellions, or gods" was also attributed to the Western Creator God. And because the theory of Buddhism does not include the concept of a Creator God, it perfectly aligns with Western atheistic thought, causing this religion, which originally had a large number of anthropomorphic gods, to instantly become atheistic and proclaim itself as such, gradually becoming a representative of science.

The concept of "God" is unclear, not just for Chinese people, but for many Westerners as well. They have misconceptions about whether God has a shape or not, and whether God should be "personified". In fact, the only incorrect perspective is seeing God as having a shape. Not to mention that you cannot find such a god, but once God is viewed as having a shape, God would lose supernatural attributes and become an ordinary material object. Can ordinary matter become God? However, many of us like to conflate these two ideas. Actually, as long as God is not regarded as having a physical form, there is some justification in "personifying" Him, because in the eyes of life, problems are inevitably viewed from the perspective of life: in the eyes of a dog, it is "dog-ification"; in the eyes of a cow, it is "cow-ification"; in the eyes of a human, it is "personification." As long as it is an abstract "character" rather than a concrete "form," there is no problem.

A river is called the mother river of a nation, which is an abstraction of the "character" of the river, but a river is not a person and must never be "shaped" into a concrete woman. Why does calling a river the mother river inspire poetic enthusiasm? This is the meaning and necessity of the abstract "personification" of the river! However, if you shape the river into a concrete "human-shaped" person, it will inevitably greatly reduce the space for lyrical expression, making it impossible for you to continue your passionate discourse, because that surging momentum is lost. And moreover, the logic is also flawed, and this error has been fully exposed among the people in those countries that worship "mud statues." They are blind and deaf, unable to discern right from wrong, indulging in superstition. This is the harm of concrete "human-shaped" personification.

If a stone trips you, you resent the stone; that is also "personifying" the stone. If you say the stone is Zhang San, a person, are you still a normal person? So "personifying God" actually looks more like a psychological necessity — it's not a question of whether you need it, but as a human you inevitably view everything in a "personified" way. If you personify everything, why oppose it when it comes to the mysterious force behind the universe? Isn't that a double standard? I find that very hard to understand!

Precisely because abstract "personification" is so crucial, such personified actions must be guided to serve the welfare of all humanity, not merely the interests of any particular class. Just as Confucianism equates "reverence for the great men and the words of the sages" with "reverence for Heaven's mandate," this effectively establishes a privileged class rather than serving the common good. Yet even Confucianism is not the worst offender. Some nations go further: though they profess belief in God, appearing deeply pious, their societies remain rigidly hierarchical, devoid of any semblance of equality among people. This piety actually channels people's worship of God covertly toward the privileged class. What they kneel before is not God, but an unequal order that facilitates the privileged class's command and control. Therefore, I do not believe that a society will necessarily become better simply because it believes in God. It depends on what the "personified God" described in their culture represents: does it primarily educate the privileged class, or does it merely educate the common people? Only the former represents the hallmark of human civilization. It must be said that to gauge a society's future, one need only examine its texts and observe how its "personified deity" instructs the privileged class—their actions and perceptions will almost certainly align with this. As for those who do not believe in God, do not fix your eyes solely on those who do. You might as well take a look at yourself; if the privileged class around you is even worse than they are, then you are no better than they are.

Humanity's unclear concept of God has existed since ancient times, and the Bible contains numerous expressions of this. The vigorous "driving away God" movement that occurred in the modern Western world is actually a recurrence of this phenomenon. This movement once again demonstrates the degree of "entropy increase" in human understanding on this matter, indicating that Westerners still lack a correct understanding of the concept of God today.

In fact, if humans do not "personify" God, they will "deify" humans, or even "shape-ify" God, both of which are a regression. Our Buddhist and Taoist religions like to "deify" humans. In Buddhism, the "Dharmakaya" of Sakyamuni is immortal and pervades the universe. This concept not only means that Buddhism does not respect logic, but also does not conform to facts, and is not a way of thinking that a normal person should have. Taoism, in addition to having the same characteristics as Buddhism, also likes to "shape-ify" God, such as shaping the Jade Emperor, shaping the Thunder God, and the Lightning Mother. It is precisely because of this difference that Taoism is often ridiculed by Buddhism as superstitious, and the word "superstition" actually came from this, which is quite ironic.

How vague and unclear humanity's concept of God is can be seen from this. And today, people regard precognitive dreams as superstition—is this not also a product of such confused thinking? Since the personified Creator God is now viewed as superstition in this age of highly advanced science, then mystical phenomena like precognitive dreams—which, like God, possess supernatural abilities—should naturally also be regarded as superstition, and thus we have the result we see today.

## 1.2.2 Does Superstition Exist Among Those Who Believe in Precognitive Dreams

Of course, it doesn't mean that those who believe in precognitive dreams are necessarily free from superstition—on the contrary, there is indeed a great deal of superstition mixed in. However, this superstition primarily exists in the beliefs of those associated with our traditional religions, yet many of us choose to turn a blind eye to it. In the late 20th century, we once exposed and criticized so-called paranormal abilities like qigong, but has anyone ever exposed or criticized the so-called supernatural powers in Buddhism and Taoism (such as divine sight, divine hearing, mind-reading, teleportation, knowledge of past lives, and liberation from defilements)? No! James Randi, founder of the U.S. Committee for Skeptical Inquiry and a magician, went so far as to pledge $1 million, held in escrow by the Goldman Foundation, to challenge claims of "supernatural abilities." He declared that the money would go to anyone who could prove they or someone else possessed such powers—and of course, no one succeeded. So why hasn't a wealthy individual in China dared to step forward and challenge these superstitious beliefs? Not only is there no such person, but I've also seen many philosophy professors—yes, professors—in our universities defending these superstitions, allowing them to thrive to this day. Take, for example(see image 04), this netizen who, after their dog died, recited the Ksitigarbha Sutra 14 times and the Rebirth Mantra 357 times simply because they dreamed of it, believing this would help the dog reincarnate sooner[2]:

---

[2] https://tieba.baidu.com/p/5104133901

有会解梦的师兄吗？可否帮我看看最后一次梦见我家狗狗…　　　　只看楼主　　收藏　　回复

我的狗狗去世快90天了，我们在一起五年了，去世后为它念了14部地藏经和357遍往生咒。在它走后60多天里一共梦见它10次，每次都是它生前和我在一起玩的样子，而距离最后一次梦见它已是20多天前，快一个月没梦见它了。
最后一次梦的内容：那是在家楼下，它突然不听话跑很快(平时都是很乖跟着人走)不回头，跑到院子花园里，突然有2只白色博美犬，我以为有一只是它，结果回头看见不是它，后来周

## Image 04

It's completely normal to dream of a deceased dog. A dog's death doesn't mean the "memory" associated with that dog in the human brain has died. If the "memory" associated with the dog died along with the dog, would that brain still be a healthy brain? Since the "memory" associated with the dog didn't die with the dog, why is it so surprising to dream of your deceased dog? It's a perfectly normal thing, yet some feel the need to recite the Ksitigarbha Sutra 14 times and the Amitabha Mantra 357 times, which is superstitious. Does anyone expose or criticize such phenomena? No! This isn't an isolated incident; such people exist in large numbers. The advent of the internet has allowed these people to expose themselves online in droves. Even today, in 2025, I still encounter many of them daily, including some highly educated individuals, such as the netizen in the link I saved earlier[3]: merely because they dreamed of a deceased friend, they went to their grave to burn paper money, believing that only then would they stop dreaming of them. How ignorant is that? It must be said that superstition indeed exists among those who believe in

---

[3] https://tieba.baidu.com/p/6232148600

precognitive dreams, and it's quite severe.

How many people mistakenly believe that the scenes in their dreams depict their past lives, leading them to firmly embrace the theory of reincarnation? How many misinterpret dreams of the deceased as messages from beyond, prompting them to burn paper offerings for salvation? How many, upon experiencing sleep paralysis, wrongly attribute it to malevolent spirits and resort to chanting spells for protection? These are the cultural barriers ingrained in us by our religious traditions—barriers that have eroded the scientific spirit in countless individuals. How many have lost their ability to think logically because of them? Superstition should rightly refer to these very beliefs, yet many turn a blind eye, instead labeling precognitive dreams as superstition and directing criticism at them. Isn't this putting the cart before the horse? This phenomenon is truly worth pondering!

1.2.3 Among those who believe in precognitive dreams, what kind of belief does not constitute superstition

So, among those who believe in precognitive dreams, what kind of belief is not superstition? Look at Confucius's example to find out. This dream was mentioned in the "life termination dream" section. According to the *Book of Rites: Tan Gong*:

Confucius had a dream before his death. In the dream, he saw himself sitting peacefully between two pillars ( refers to the pillars in front of a main hall), receiving offerings of wine and food. The next day, he told Zigong, 'I am probably going to die.' Zigong didn't believe him, so Confucius explained that people in the Xia dynasty, when they died, were placed on the eastern steps; people in the Zhou dynasty, when they died, were placed on the western steps; but people in the Yin dynasty, when they died, were placed between two pillars. And I am a descendant of the Yin people, sitting between two pillars receiving sacrifices. I certainly won't live for many more days. Indeed, Confucius passed away just seven days later.

Confucius was a descendant of the Yin people, and the custom of the Yin people was to place the dead between two pillars for sacrificial rites. Based on this logic, Confucius believed this dream was a sign of his imminent death. There is nothing particularly special about Confucius's interpretation; he simply connected it to his reality, and dreams are about a person's reality. This means that as long as one finds the reality associated with the dream, the dream is essentially interpreted. Such a method of dream interpretation is clear in its origin and process, with its correctness easily discernible. Even if misinterpreted, it would merely be a judgment error that could be promptly corrected.

From Confucius's approach to dream interpretation, it's evident that he was quite skilled, truly befitting a historical figure - someone else might have missed such insights. The author's approach to dream interpretation is similar to Confucius's, with nothing particularly unique, but it must be objective, practical, and based on evidence. If misinterpreted, one should be able to find the reason for the error. Such an approach with a clear process, result, and ability to trace back to the source, using facts as a standard, cannot be considered superstitious. Buddhism and Taoism's explanations are different; their interpretations are even more illusory than the dream itself, with their cause-and-effect relationships established in previous and future lives, disconnected from this world and fundamentally impossible to verify - which is superstitious.

It appears that people's perception of precognitive dreams as superstitious is a product of cognitive confusion, without clearly understanding whether the phenomenon of precognitive dreams itself is superstitious or if the process of interpreting such a phenomenon involves superstition. Is it acknowledging precognitive dreams as superstitious, or are certain distortions superstitious? Therefore, when people say precognitive dreams are superstitious, they actually don't understand what they're saying. Their thinking is chaotic, their understanding is low, much like how they oppose God without clearly understanding the definition of God - they are like "a frog in a well who doesn't know the sea, a summer insect who doesn't know ice, a scholar who doesn't understand the Tao."

**Multiple-Choice questions:**

32

The following belong to idol Baal (        ); belong to human-shaped gods (          ); belong to human-shaped things (          ); belong to personified gods (          ); belong to personified things (          ); belong to deified humans (          ); belong to deified behaviors (          ); belong to deified data (          ).

1.  Incantation.

2.  Consecration (Buddhist/Taoist ceremony).

3.  Luck. god;

4.  Ba Zi.

5.  Bodhisattva.

6.  Tathagata.

7.  Shen Wuhua (Incarnation of Guanyin Bodhisattva).

8.  The Jade Emperor of Taoism.

9.  The candle turns to ash, and only then do the tears dry.

10. Meeting is a kind of destiny.

11. Justice has a long arm; though the net is wide, it lets nothing through.

12. Justice may be late, but it is never absent.

13. Kuafu chasing the sun, Nüwa patching the sky, Hou Yi shooting the suns.

14. If I do not enter hell, who will? Only when all sentient beings are saved will enlightenment be attained. I vow not to become a Buddha until hell is empty.

15. The law of the Lord is perfect, reviving the soul; the

statutes of the Lord are trustworthy, making wise the simple.

16.  A row of willows is half-submerged in the water, looking like a group of young girls lifting their skirts to wash their long hair under the moonlight.

## 1.3 Hallucination Theory's Objections to Precognitive Dreams

Hallucination theory, also known as "hallucination memory theory," is another negative statement about precognitive dreams that follows the coincidence theory and the theory of superstition. On Baidu Encyclopedia, entering "hallucination memory" will directly jump to "déjà vu," and "déjà vu" is also explained as "hallucination memory," meaning they are equivalent. This explanation was first proposed by the French physiologist Émile Boirac in 1876, which is of course a big mistake.

Déjà vu, literally meaning "already seen," manifests as an individual suddenly feeling that certain scenes they are experiencing have been encountered before, a sense of "familiarity." In short, it's the feeling of "familiarity" with something or a scene that has never been experienced before, as if it had been experienced at some time and place. Research reports indicate that at least two-thirds of people have had this experience, often manifesting in the following three situations:

When entering a new environment, it feels as if I've been there before.

For something that just happened, there's suddenly an inexplicable sense of familiarity.

Such scenes seem to have appeared in dreams before.

For the first case, the current explanation is: this is because the brain misprocesses information, mistakenly treating the present input as or judging it to be a "picture from memory."

For the second case, the current explanation is: from a medical perspective, this is caused by a sudden miscoordination in information processing between the left and right hemispheres of the brain, causing something briefly seen during vision to be mistaken for something seen in the past.

For the third case, the current explanation is: the so-called appearance in a dream is actually a hallucination, because it is merely a scene similar to the past, provided or activated by the dream.

The above explanation is still relatively neutral, and there is an extreme explanation that it is a disease. Since "déjà vu" is characterized as an illusion, it means that "déjà vu" is an unreal and abnormal feeling, so it is logical to interpret it as a mental illness. A psychology professor and doctoral supervisor at Peking University said: "Déjà vu occurs in everyone, but if this feeling is too frequent and too strong, it is a pathology." In fact, on the contrary, having this experience is not only not pathological, but also normal, indicating that such a person's brain is operating efficiently, and if the signal is very strong, it means that the brain is in optimal operation. If they happen to be in danger at this time, such people are the most likely to escape. It is really shocking to me that such an argument has appeared in our higher education institutions. Not only this mentor, but I also noticed that some parents take their children to the hospital for examination because their children's phenomenon is too strong, and the advice given by the doctor's message on the Internet is to let the child go to the hospital neurology department for examination. These doctors are supposed to represent the cutting edge of our academic community, yet their advice is conveying wrong information to society.

Of course, it cannot be completely ruled out that there is indeed a possibility of hallucinations, after all, a person does have a mental trance, but there is still a big difference between "mental trance" and "sense of déjà vu", and it is not difficult to distinguish. It is believed that most of the sense of déjà vu is related to precognitive dreams, because the foundation of consciousness originates from dreams, and dreams are the source code of consciousness - this view will eventually be proven.

Not everyone's "déjà vu" is vague; many people are quite clear about whether their memories are hallucinations, which provides evidence for determining whether "déjà vu" originates from "paramnesia." Below is a dream example related to love, posted by a netizen named "Night Sky Purple Star" on January 27, 2017, describing a sense of "déjà vu" she experienced when her boyfriend visited her home for the first time during their relationship. From this example, you can see how unreliable the claim is that "so-called appearances in dreams are merely similar scenes from the past, with dreams providing or activating these memories":

My boyfriend and I started dating in September 2016. During the holiday in October, my parents weren't home. <u>The first reaction he had when he came to my house for the first time was that it felt very familiar. Later, he remembered a dream he had a few days before, in which he had dreamed of my house.</u>

I had only video chatted with him in my room before, but the scene he dreamed of was almost identical to the layout of my home, except for some differences in the TV and refrigerator. In the dream, we were already married and seemed to have children. We went to my home together to visit my parents. My dad wasn't home at the time, and my mom said she had gone to pick up our grandson...

In my dream, the refrigerator in my house was a Siemens double-door model, but in reality, when he came in October, we had an old refrigerator that had been in use for ten years. But just a couple of days ago, our refrigerator broke down. My parents went out to buy a new one, but I didn't go with them because I went to see a movie with him. When I got home that night... there was a double-door refrigerator. Honestly, it doesn't quite match our old house.

I didn't realize it that night, but this morning I suddenly remembered that my partner had said the refrigerator he dreamed about was different from ours. I asked him what kind of refrigerator it was. He said, "It's a double-door one, but yours isn't." I sent him a photo. He asked, "Is it a Siemens?" I said, "Yes!" He said, "I dreamed about Siemens in the dream." I was stunned. Although the dream wasn't one hundred percent accurate, the layout of our home is getting closer and closer to the layout of the home in that dream, and I didn't manipulate it at all[4].

The underlined part is a form of "déjà vu." When the dreamer visited his girlfriend's home for the first time, it also triggered a sense of familiarity, suddenly recalling a dream, which could rule out the possibility of it being a hallucination. This dream didn't come true all at once, but in two parts, with the second part definitely occurring in the future, thus confirming it as a

---

[4] https://tieba.baidu.com/p/4957273291

precognitive dream: first was the sense of familiarity, as if having been there before - that was the first part; then came the refrigerator - that was the second part. The dreamer described this dream before it came true, and since it came true after his description, this disproves the critics' claim that "it's merely a scenario similar to past experiences, with the dream providing or activating these memories" - since this doesn't hold true, it's not a hallucination - since it's not a hallucination, it means the dreamer had actually rehearsed it in the dream, and the sense of familiarity becomes equivalent to experiencing it for the second time (first in the dream, second in reality) - since it's the second time, when it happens in reality, the feeling of déjà vu can occur. This is the truth! Most people who have this experience experience it in the same way, only some remember their dreams while others don't, which leads to variations in the "déjà vu" experience. If you recall the "clip-clop of horse hooves" dream I mentioned earlier, my feeling at that time was very clear and very special.

In summary, "déjà vu" is actually a psychological phenomenon triggered by dreams, an "overflow" of dreams that can intensify consciousness, not an illusion. People explaining it as an illusion is likely a reluctant choice, a last resort, because until the truth is revealed, that's the only way you can explain it. Otherwise, how could you find a better explanation? Since no one accepts precognitive dreams, explaining it as an illusion becomes the only correct choice. What does "what exists is reasonable" mean? This is probably it, because you can only explain it this way; there are no other options, because other options, the correct ones, have already been blocked by you. In this case, the wrong explanation becomes the correct one, and the illusion becomes the truth.

The opponents' explanation of déjà vu as a hallucinatory memory is more like a group of people who have never experienced it trying to guide a group of people who have. Their answers are like "frogs in a well," "summer insects," and "narrow-minded scholars" discussing an unknown world. They know nothing about the unknown world, yet they act as if they know everything. In this way, people's understanding of this issue is bound to be mistakenly influenced by these individuals. However, some people have shown recognition for the idea that "déjà vu originates from precognitive dreams." I've seen online that Swiss scientist Arthur Finkhauser believes this, but such people are rare and cannot make any significant impact. Given this, the only theory that can gain widespread acceptance is the "illusion theory."

**Short-answer question:**

For this dream example, which plot point is most likely to be misunderstood by the dreamer? Please underline it.

# 1.4 Temporal Indeterminacy Theory's Objections to Precognitive Dreams

The theory of temporal indeterminacy refers to a critical argument against precognitive dreams, wherein opponents contend that the fulfillment of dream content in future real-world events lacks temporal constraints. It posits that such fulfillment is not bound by clear, verifiable time limits, allowing for arbitrary selection of the "fulfillment window."

Critics argue that a claimed precognitive dream, whose "fulfillment timing" often relies on vague temporal descriptions and flexible matching, has an infinitely open time window. It could happen the day after waking, next month, or even years later, allowing any event at any time to be forcibly linked: if someone dreams of a "disaster," a traffic accident hours later or an earthquake years later could both be interpreted as "fulfillment." This temporal vagueness and arbitrary time matching mean that any current "unfulfillment" cannot refute a precognitive dream, as proponents can always claim "the time has not yet come." However, once a specific date is given, it falls apart, as seen with Japanese manga artist Ryo Tatsuki's failed prediction of a major earthquake and tsunami in Japan on July 5, 2025. If precognitive dreams truly exist, why can't they be precisely predicted?

Indeed, if the fulfillment of precognitive dreams were as arbitrary as critics suggest, their skepticism would be unassailable.

However, is this truly the case? I have repeatedly emphasized this point in the previous three volumes: for either side, pro or con, to have a correct conclusion, they must first understand how dreams work. If they cannot, it's like "chickens talking to ducks," and no one can get to the heart of the matter.

Precognitive dreams are divided into direct dreams and symbolic dreams. Direct dreams are rare, yet many of Ryo Tatsuki's predictions were formed from direct dreams. The question is, were all of his "direct dreams" truly "direct dreams"? Is there no possibility that some were "symbolic dreams"? Even if probability were exceptionally kind to him, he could at most exceed the average level; how could all of them be direct? As long as it's a symbolic dream, errors in interpretation are inevitable; otherwise, the secret of dreams would not remain unrevealed to this day.

Such instances of proponents making mistakes are not uncommon. In the third volume, I mentioned many examples, including an experiment conducted by an Israeli person who, based solely on the appearance of the word "carbide" in someone's dream, concluded that the dream was related to an explosion at an Indian chemical plant. This is far too far-fetched, and calling such a dream a precognitive dream is undoubtedly "shooting oneself in the foot."

The affirmative side has problems, and so does the negative side. The negative side's opposition to the affirmative is like the affirmative saying, "Sand is gold," and the negative then concluding, "Gold doesn't exist." Instead of considering that the affirmative's statement might be wrong, the negative directly uses it to prove that "gold doesn't exist"—because the affirmative said "sand is gold." The result is that the affirmative constantly provides poor evidence, undermining the credibility of its own viewpoint, while the negative, by refuting this poor evidence, gains a "self-validating" illusion that it is always right. Both sides believe they are justified, yet unknowingly bury the truth together in the sand.

The truth is: far from being arbitrary and vague as critics claim, the fulfillment times of precognitive dreams are actually very clear and specific. Even when there are delays, they follow a distinct exponential decay pattern, not without regularity. The distribution of fulfillment times for the 23 dreams I introduced in Volume II serves as excellent evidence:

On the first day, 11 were fulfilled, accounting for 48%;

On the second day, 2 were fulfilled, accounting for 9%;

On the third day, 3 were fulfilled, accounting for 13%;

From the fourth day to one week, 4 were fulfilled, accounting for 17%;

About half a month, 2 were fulfilled, accounting for 9%;

Over one year, 1 was fulfilled, accounting for 4%.

Nearly half were fulfilled on the first day, and 87% within a week. This is not an isolated case; the first volume mentioned 24 "fighting dreams" and "killing dreams," and the distribution of their fulfillment times was similar, with half fulfilled on the first day and 87% within a week. The delay in their fulfillment also shows a clear exponential decay trend, not without pattern:

On the first day, 12 were fulfilled, accounting for 50%;

On the second day, 4 were fulfilled, accounting for 17%;

On the third day, 2 were fulfilled, accounting for 8%;

From the fourth day to one week, 3 were fulfilled, accounting for 13%;

Around half a month, 2 were fulfilled, accounting for 8%;

Over one month, 1 was fulfilled, accounting for 5%.

Below is a detailed distribution of the 24 "fighting dreams" and "killing dreams" in terms of their fulfillment times:

(1) On the first day, 12 came true, accounting for 50%

1)  I killed a person, and his partner was willing to be killed by me as well.

2)  A street vendor killed my mother's dance partner with a knife.

3)  A group of aliens descending from a UFO accidentally killed one of their own while chasing and trying to kill me.

4)  I killed two men cleanly and decisively with a knife.

5)  I provoked a confrontation and was surrounded, but was powerless to fight back.

44

6)  I watched both sides of a battle digging tunnels to attack each other.

7)  I and a group of people were hunted down by aliens descending from the sky.

8)  I twisted a person into a pretzel shape.

9)  My cousin and I gunned down a group of enemies, but we didn't see any bodies.

10)  I used a shovel to pound a person into the ground like a wedge.

11)  Someone I offended brought reinforcements to take revenge on me, but it turned out we knew each other, and we reconciled.

12)  I killed several people with a shovel and sticks.

(2) On the next day, 4 came true, accounting for 17%

1)  I fell for a woman's "self-injury scheme".

2)  The newly appointed boss killed his predecessor, only to be killed by my cousin.

3)  A man managed to escape the fate of being killed by me.

4)  There were two men whose stomachs were incredibly tough—I couldn't stab through them with a knife.

(3) On the third day, 2 came true, accounting for 8%

1)  I successfully tripped someone who was attacking me, sending them to the ground.

2)  I drove away three people who tried to enter my house.

(4) From the fourth day to one week, 3 were fulfilled, accounting for 13%

1)  I took advantage of my cousin's inattention and killed him with a sword.

2)  A group of pigs were arguing like humans, and one of them got badly beaten, with its face covered in blood.

3)  A fellow soldier helped me deal with another troublemaking comrade.

(5) About half a month later, 2 came true, accounting for 8%

1)  Someone stole my money and then stabbed me.

2)  I killed a rabbit; after the rabbit became a person, I killed it again.

(6) More than one month: 1 fulfillment, accounting for 5%

1)  I was chased and killed by a motorcyclist.

The distribution of fulfillment times for other precognitive dreams is similar; they generally come true within a few days and don't drag on for too long. Dreams that take a very long time to be fulfilled are individual cases. However, even these individual cases follow certain rules and are not arbitrary. Furthermore, in terms of sample randomness, the dream examples above also meet statistical requirements. The first time involved all samples within a month, and the second time involved "same type" samples. These two statistical methods can represent randomness under different conditions, belonging to multiple dimensions, and can fully be used as evidence. There are many such examples, which will be explained in detail later, and in terms of patterns, they are all pretty much the same, and this is also the prototype of the second law of dreams or precognitive dreams.

The specific fulfillment of the first 23 dreams was already introduced in the second volume. As for these 24 dreams, they are only briefly introduced here, as there is a dedicated volume for them later. Regarding these dreams, why not try to imagine how they actually came true? Without comparing them to reality, you could rack your brain and still never imagine why they, too, are precognitive dreams. You would inevitably be left scratching your head; however, once you learn the truth, you will understand why the voices opposing precognitive dreams prevail. The answer is that humans are constrained by their cognitive limitations, unable to perceive anything beyond those bounds. The phrase "a frog at the bottom of a well" is no exaggeration.

**Multiple-choice questions:**

Regarding the 24 "fighting dreams" and "killing dreams" mentioned in this article, the attitude or method for determining whether they are precognitive dreams is:

1.    Perhaps I'm wrong, and I'm willing to see what the author

says.

2. I'm willing to bet against the author; if I'm wrong, I'm willing to pay the equivalent price.

3. "Drawing a gourd after seeing one," comparing the author's dream with my own dream can reveal whether the author is right or wrong.

4. Check whether it conforms to the most basic laws of dreams proposed by the author, using the author's spear to strike the author's shield.

5. Science has proven that precognitive dreams do not exist, and what's more, the author claims that "all dreams are precognitive," so there is no need to read it at all.

## 1.5 Psychology's Objections to Precognitive Dreams

Psychology's objections to precognitive dreams essentially perpetuates Freud's negative stance on the phenomenon. This is particularly true within China's psychological community, where Freud's influence remains so dominant that he is practically revered as an unchallenged authority! This stems from the fact that, from a psychological perspective, dreams serve as a tool for studying individual psychological tool created by Freud. As such, psychology can never acknowledge the existence of precognitive dreams, for doing so would undermine the functionality of this tool and threaten their "iron rice bowl." Therefore, redefining psychology's understanding of dreams can only be driven by seemingly insignificant innovators from other dimensions, the academic community itself lacks the capacity for self-revolution.

## 1.5.1 Freud's Negative Interpretation of Precognitive Dreams

Freud's negative interpretation of precognitive dreams shares similarities and differences with both the superstition theory and the coincidence theory. The similarity lies in their mutual rejection of precognitive dreams and disbelief in their ability to foretell the future. The difference is that while Freud denies the existence of precognitive dreams and their predictive power, he acknowledges their significance. He interprets this meaning as stemming from past unconscious desires, serving to fulfill wish satisfaction. Freud stated, "The future depicted in dreams is not entirely devoid of authenticity," and "Dreams do indeed lead us toward the future," but only "by presenting wish fulfillment as a path to the future." This implies that while a dream may seem to foretell the future, it is not genuinely prophetic, "for all dreams originate from the past." "this future is cast in the mold of the past by indestructible desires." Therefore, the "value of precognitive dreams for the future is a question that cannot be established," and one should replace the "understanding of the future in precognitive dreams with an understanding of the past." In other words, the driving force of dreams lies in the past[5].

At the beginning of Chapter 7 of *The Interpretation of Dreams*, there is a dream example of precognitive dreams, which Freud quotes many times to explain how a person's dreams are influenced by the past to fulfill a person's wishes. It was a precognitive dream in a lecturer's lecture relayed by one of his patients, which was thought to have foretold the occurrence of a fire, but the lecturer disagreed:

> A father hired an old man to keep watch for his newly deceased child. Candles were lit all around the child. He himself slept in a nearby room. To be able to see the child's room, he left the door open. Then he had the following dream: In the dream, his newly deceased child stood by his bedside, grabbing his arm and shouting, "Dad, didn't you see I'm on fire?" Startled awake, the father immediately ran to check and found the old man who was keeping watch had fallen asleep. A tilted candle had just burned the bedsheet and the child's arm.

In fact, this is simply a precognitive dream, nothing more, yet our psychology researchers insist on being unconventional to highlight their uniqueness. From the lecturer's perspective, the father dreamed of a fire because his eyes had caught the glow of

---

[5] (Austria) Sigmund Freud, *The Interpretation of Dreams*, translated by Zhang Yanyun, Liaoning People's Publishing House, 1987, p. 579

flames in the child's room, combined with his doubts about whether the elderly could properly care for the child, which led to such a dream. Freud strongly agreed with the lecturer's interpretation, stating: "All dreams under unconscious desires are supported by the wish to sleep[6]." This wish is related to the father's desire for his child to live a little longer in the dream, hence the continuation of the dream. The child's words in the dream—"Daddy, don't you see I'm burning?"—likely connect to a past event, such as the child having a high fever before death.

The idiom "qiān qiáng fù huì" (stretching the meaning, making forced interpretations) means to insist that something has a certain meaning when it doesn't, or to forcibly link unrelated things and confuse them. Freud's explanation is precisely this, for three reasons:

First, if the child's father truly knew the light was caused by a fire, he would have immediately rushed out; it's impossible he would have waited. This would be true from both a reflexive and a conscious perspective. The only reason he didn't rush out is that he was currently asleep and couldn't comprehend that the light was caused by a fire. A person who is asleep cannot have judgment; if they do have judgment, it can only be after they wake up. This is the truth.

---

[6] (Austria) Sigmund Freud, *The Interpretation of Dreams*, translated by Qing Run, Taiwan Publishing House, 1987, p. 421

Second, as everyone knows, people in their sleep perceive dreams as reality, and this dream is no different. In this dream, the child's father didn't know the child had died, so how could he intentionally keep himself from waking up just to spend more time with the child in the dream? Moreover, people cannot control their dreams. How could the child's father manage to stay longer just because he wanted to? If a person could truly do whatever they wanted in a dream, wouldn't they be able to fully enjoy themselves when they met someone they liked in a dream? But the fact is that dreams are spontaneous and not controlled by people. When they start and when they end is entirely up to the dream. Clearly, this is an untenable answer.

Third, if the child's father was indeed stimulated by the light, it could also have been a bonfire or someone making a fire to cook. Why must it be a fire disaster? This possibility cannot be ruled out, yet Freud chose to ignore it.

It's clear how strained Freud's explanation was. In contrast, explaining it as a precognitive dream requires no such complexity; it simply manifested in reality, and immediately so. It's so straightforward, yet they insist on such convoluted reasoning, getting themselves and others confused. You don't have to believe in precognitive dreams, but your explanation should at least be more reasonable and simpler than the precognitive dream explanation to be plausible, right? But clearly, psychological researchers have not only failed to do so but have also acted quite childishly. The reason for this is that a precognitive dream is simply a precognitive dream; no further explanation is needed, otherwise, it's just gilding the lily!

## 1.5.2 Freud's Denial of Precognitive Dreams is Itself the Fulfillment of a Wish

In fact, it's not that dreams are wish fulfillment, but rather that Freud's denial of precognitive dreams is itself a wish fulfillment. Of course, this is also a common characteristic of everyone influenced by Freud. This isn't a jest; it's a fact, clearly written in his behavior. You'll find that he's deeply entrenched and unable to extricate himself. "Using your spear to attack your shield!" If we analyze Freud's view on precognitive dreams using his own theory of wish fulfillment, it won't be difficult to discover traces of this wish fulfillment in his beliefs and work.

In the 19th century, a wave of expelling God swept across the West, and Freud was the vanguard of that era. Some commented, "Freud's greatest contribution was to liberate human thought from God!" The Bible views precognitive dreams as originating from God the Creator, belonging to the supernatural, which he absolutely could not accept. Freud once said with concern, "We would be wrong to assume that in our time no one supports the theory that dreams originate from the supernatural. Before science clears away these remnants, besides the devout and mystical writers who still cling to the once prevalent supernatural realm, we often find that very clear-headed people, while opposing any fanciful notions in other respects, devoutly believe in the existence and convergence of supernatural spiritual forces in the mysterious nature of dreams[7]." From his words, one can see how resistant Freud was to acknowledging the existence of the supernatural, calling these people "remnants of an atheistic age"! Why Freud said this is precisely related to his deep-seated unconscious desires.

As an atheist, if he doesn't completely deny the authenticity of precognitive dreams, it would be tantamount to admitting the existence of supernatural powers, which contradicts his worldview. Therefore, he must oppose them. Isn't this precisely his deep-seated desire for wish fulfillment at play? Why Freud opposed precognitive dreams is now crystal clear! This means his view on precognitive dreams was not born out of thoughtful rationality, but out of emotional sensibility, a sensibility that completely severed his rationality from the truth.

From Freud's work, one can also see the fulfillment of this desire within him. Freud studied dreams not to unravel their secrets but rather to find a pathway toward solving mental illnesses. In his own words, it was "to pave the way for the study of the more

---

[7] (Austria) Sigmund Freud, *The Interpretation of Dreams*, translated by Qing Run, Taiwan Publishing House, 1987, p. 3

obscure psychology of the neuroses by interpreting dreams[8]," this was his fundamental objective. Therefore, rather than saying Freud was researching dreams, it would be more accurate to say he was using dreams to achieve his own goals, which were tied to his profession as a psychiatrist. His work involved using dreams as a conversational entry point to break through barriers in communication with patients, uncovering their private thoughts, and thus providing material for his "therapeutic dialogue." In his hands, dreams were merely a tool he employed.

The research method for precognitive dreams involves seeking clues from the future, which prevents the discovery of past clues from a patient's history. However, a patient's past clues are crucial for diagnosing their condition. For this reason, Freud could only oppose precognitive dreams. Yet, because he wanted to utilize dreams, he had to acknowledge that all dreams have meaning, including precognitive dreams. Thus, "dreams are a completely reasonable psychic phenomenon[9]" became a conclusion he was forced to draw. At this point, it becomes clear why Freud first denied precognitive dreams and then gave them a positive evaluation: the root cause was "wish fulfillment"! Although his theory does not apply to dreams, it is highly applicable to his

---

[8] (Austria) Sigmund Freud, *The Interpretation of Dreams*, translated by Zhang Yanyun, Liaoning People's Publishing House, 1987, p. 96

[9] (Austria) Sigmund Freud, *The Interpretation of Dreams*, translated by Zhang Yanyun, Liaoning People's Publishing House, 1987, p. 114

research process, which is a great irony!

## 1.5.3 Freud's Significance for China and the West

It must be admitted that Freud does have a certain positive significance for China: at the very least he can erect a firewall in our traditional culture, keeping the eerie explanations of Buddhism and Daoism that can seize the mind and steal the soul out of the classroom, allowing our students to view things from an apparently more objective standpoint and no longer treat their dreams by reciting sutras, burning paper, or performing afterlife rites. Although many people remain obstinately ignorant—preferring to burn joss paper, put on airs about spirits, and despise the God who rebukes such peculiar behaviors—at least a wedge has been driven into their midst, providing a bit more fertile ground for those who still have some capacity for thought, giving them another choice and a chance to breathe, otherwise the whole nation would surely be annihilated.

Freud has had little positive significance for the West; on the contrary, he has been somewhat destructive. This is because Western understanding of dreams is primarily influenced by Christianity, while in China it is mainly influenced by Buddhism and Taoism. The former largely aligns with the research findings of this book, while the latter completely contradicts them. This indicates that Freud has played a destructive role in the West but a therapeutic role in China. The same matter, different outcomes—

truly "a tiny error leads to a huge discrepancy!" Fortunately, the West has a political environment that allows freedom of speech and a relaxed academic atmosphere. As long as one is not "firing blanks," making unfounded statements, and demonstrates responsibility, anyone is permitted and encouraged to freely express their views:

"Freud's theory itself is actually a scientific nightmare, and it's time to wake up from it[10]." Some people commented like this.

"Freud is the most amazing and arrogant intellectual hoax of the twentieth century!" British Nobel Prize winner Meadow said.

With such diverse voices, their negative impact could be minimized to the lowest level. However, in China, there are almost only words of praise. Shouldn't our academic world be a place of a hundred schools of thought contending? This is definitely not what a civilized society should have. No wonder when I consulted certain publishing units about publication matters, they replied to me like this: "Freud's books can be published, but yours cannot!" Isn't this practice of exclusively revering authority a form of spiritual conservatism and regression? Their approach not only stifles the vitality of academic innovation but also departs from the spirit of openness and inclusivity they advocate; it not only harms the innovators themselves but also brings shame upon the entire collective. They once used Freud to break tradition, yet now they

---

[10] Myers, David. *Psychology*, 7th ed. Translated by Huang Xiting. p. 236

have turned him into a new tradition, prepared to carry it forward. They are themselves lazy in reflection and intolerant of reflection from others.

**Short-answer question:**

Please analyze the reasons for Freud's success in China from the aspects of timing, geographical advantage, and human harmony?

# Section 2: Supporters' Misconceptions of Precognitive Dreams

If you think that only opponents will create obstacles to revealing the truth about precognitive dreams, you would be greatly mistaken. In fact, those supporters pose the same problem. Such theories as the posthumous dream communication theory, the anti-dream theory, divination, mysticism theory, and the past-life theory discussed in the first volume—these theories proposed by supporters have not only failed to advance the revelation of precognitive dreams' truth, but have actually complicated the matter. They not only provide reasons for superstitious believers to justify their superstitions, but also mislead opponents into believing their views are correct, making the emergence of truth increasingly impossible.

## 2.1 Posthumous Dream Communication Theory's Misconceptions of Precognitive Dreams

### 2.1.1 The Rationality and Flaws of the Posthumous Dream Communication Theory

Posthumous dream communication, superstitious interpretation, refers to the act of transmitting information to the living in a dream when the deceased has an unfulfilled wish.

"Posthumous Dream Communication Theory" primarily exists among people within the cultural background of Buddhism and Taoism. This concept is not merely about dream interpretation; it is actually a matter concerning belief and worldview. This is because once a person is influenced by "Posthumous Dream Communication Theory," they unconsciously accept the following ideas:

after death, people still live in the underworld, and they only die in the flesh. As for the dream itself, since such a dream is tantamount to "foreknowing" the current situation of the deceased or matters in the underworld, it is also similar to a precognitive dream, but it is not a precognitive dream as the author says, but a "pseudo-precognitive dream". However, "existence is reasonable", human beings believe that the existence of "posthumous dream communication" is not completely unreasonable, but this truth is not the truth, but a misunderstanding, which is determined by the illusory nature and complexity of dreams, so traces of this statement can be seen in various cultures, but there are differences in the amount of ink and the degree of superstition - Christianity has the least ink, basically one stroke, and the degree of superstition is the slightest; Buddhism and Taoism have the most ink, big books, and the words are not amazing and endless, and the degree of superstition is the most serious, moreover, Buddhism has incorporated it into its scriptures, having followers recite and copy it repeatedly like first-grade students, thereby solidifying it as a belief, making its influence far from ordinary.

Here are three specific examples that make it hard to disbelieve the existence of the "posthumous dream communication phenomenon," otherwise dreams wouldn't be so consistent with the facts, especially the first two dreams that helped the police solve the cases.

(1) Jilin Police Solve Murder Case Based on Victim's " Dream Visitation" to Sister

On November 27, 2014, CCTV's "Sai Beining Time" aired a program called "Capturing the Culprit through Dreams", which described how police successfully solved a murder case caused by a love triangle through a "dream visitation". In June 2008, the Public Security Bureau of Changbai Mountain in Jilin Province received a report from villagers who found a bloodstained garment near their doorstep, suspecting a neighbor had been murdered. However, with no body found, the case was shelved. A few days later, the victim's sister approached the police, saying she dreamed her brother told her he was buried in a bush 20 meters from the railway near their home. The police, with a skeptical attitude, went to search the location and indeed unearthed the victim's body, thus enabling progress in the case.

(2) Vietnamese Police Solve Case Based on Deceased's "Dream

Visitation" to Mother

Vietnamese media reported on April 20, 2019, that a few days prior, a mother in Yen Bai Province, Vietnam, dreamt that her daughter, who had been missing for two months, was crying in a desolate well. Following the dream, she went to search near her son-in-law's house and indeed found her daughter's body in a well. The victim, Pham Thi H, 30 years old, originally lived with her husband in Hung Thinh Village, Yen Bai Province. Two months earlier, Pham's mother could not contact her, but her son-in-law insisted she had gone to work elsewhere. As days passed, the mother's worry grew, and then for several consecutive days, she dreamt of her daughter crying in a desolate well. She then checked all the wells near her son-in-law's house and finally found her daughter's decomposed body in a dry well, at which point the truth came to light.

(3) Relatives Discover the Deceased's Grave Has Been Flooded Through the " Dream Visitation" of the Deceased

Here is the text from the screenshot(image 05): "I dreamed that my late grandmother said her feet were cold. My father hurried to her grave to burn shoes as an offering, only to find that water from construction work at the cemetery above had flowed into my grandmother's grave."

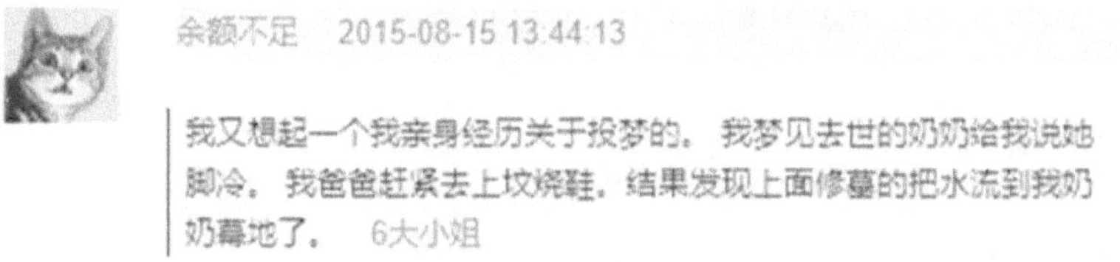

Image 05

From this it can be seen that the widely circulated "posthumous dream communication phenomenon" is not baseless. The saying "what exists is reasonable" seems to have some merit, but that doesn't necessarily mean it is truly valid — it may simply reflect limitations in people's understanding. If that's the case, then "what exists is reasonable" is not necessarily reasonable. Whether it is reasonable depends on whether a " posthumous dream communication " is the only explanation: if it is the only explanation, then the "posthumous dream communication theory" is reasonable and correct; if it is not the only explanation and there are other possibilities, then the "posthumous dream communication theory" has flaws, is unreasonable, and needs further verification. The fact is, if the "posthumous dream communication phenomenon" is regarded as a precognitive dream, like other precognitive dreams, it's simply dreaming rather than the deceased "posthumous dream communication," and that makes just as much sense.

Taking the first and second examples, we can also consider this to be an ability of the dream itself. For these two dream scenes, "the deceased informing" and "the deceased crying in the well," we can also consider them to be a form of symbolic expression adopted by the dream for the sake of "plot" needs, in order to reveal the truth, rather than the deceased appearing in a "posthumous dream communication." This is very likely, because similar scenes are frequently seen in other dreams as well; simply calling them "posthumous dream communication" because the person is dead is itself unreasonable.

In news reports, Mr. Li, a lottery player from Hunan, won 7.78 million RMB based on a string of numbered balls thrown to him by someone in his dream. Does this mean that person was "dream visitation" to him? Mr. Wei, a lottery player from Shaanxi, dreamed of the "God of Wealth" and won 6 million RMB—does this imply the "God of Wealth" truly exists? A woman dreamed of a "license plate number" and won 10.5 million RMB—does this suggest the license plate was "dream visitation" to her? Of course not. These are merely analogies to illustrate that the dreamer would win a big prize. In reality, it's just a precognitive dream—nothing more than dreaming about it. However, simply because the deceased appeared in the dream, people become confused, start overthinking, and fabricate wild stories.

As for the third example, we can also understand it as a kind of precognitive ability of dreams, which is the dream that knows the situation in the cemetery of the deceased relatives across time and space, and as for the plot in the dream "the deceased says that his feet are cold", we can also regard it as an image deliberately created to reveal what happened in reality, and there is no need to use "posthumous dream communication" to explain it. If it has to be interpreted in this way, there will be contradictions in the interpretation of other dreams, and there will be "double standards".

It can be seen that although the "posthumous dream communication theory" has a certain rationality, it is not really reasonable, and it is regarded as a precognitive dream - just seeing it in a dream, which is also reasonable. This shows that there are loopholes in the "posthumous dream communication theory", and to regard the "posthumous dream communication phenomenon" as the dead must be "posthumous dream communication" is to make the mistake of generalizing like the book *Zhou Gong Interpretation of Dreams*.

Moreover, the error of the "posthumous dream communication theory" can also be discovered statistically. In psychology, this is known as "confirmation bias," which refers to the powerful, unconscious tendency we all have to seek out, notice, accept, and remember information that confirms our pre-existing beliefs, while ignoring, doubting, or forgetting information that contradicts them. Simply put, we are more likely to remember the instances where "I was right" and ignore the evidence where "I was wrong." The reality is that if you examine all "dreams of the deceased" together, you will find that the dream cases that do not fit the "posthumous dream communication theory" are the vast majority, while those that seem to fit are the rare minority. It is precisely this rare minority that receives special attention and is remembered, becoming evidence that the deceased are "visiting in dreams." For example, the dreams I collected below stray far from the "posthumous dream communication theory," yet people pretend not to see them:

(1) Although he passed away more than a month ago, I dreamed he was dying again.

(2) My deceased father was cutting my hair; to make me behave, my family held me down.

(3) I dreamed my late great-grandmother was trying to kill me. I asked her why; she said she had no money left to spend.

(4) My mother dreamed that my deceased father got into a fight with someone and was taken away by the police, who told her to pay a ransom.

(5) It's been 28 days since my father died in a car accident. The day before yesterday I dreamed he came out of the morgue and said to me, "It's okay now, let's go home!"

(6) The first moment I saw her in the dream, I thought, Didn't she die? Why is she standing in front of me? She reached out her hand toward me and asked if she could have my eyes. I was very

scared and said no!

(7) The day after my dad died, I dreamed he told me he was in a suspended death; later I dreamed he told me he was working as a gatekeeper at a factory; today I dreamed he cooked a meal of dumplings and small wontons for my mother and me.

(8) It's been almost ten years since my dad died from illness, and I rarely dream about him. A few nights ago I dreamed he was in the living room looking for something to eat. My maternal grandparents heard the noise and went to check the living room; he was going to harm them. My mother and I hid in the bedroom and called the police.

(9) I dreamed that my deceased grandfather was still alive. We knew he had already passed, and we all hid it from him. Later, someone accidentally let it slip and he found out, and he smiled and said goodbye to us.

These nine examples differ markedly from the three above and are fundamentally unlike "Posthumous dream communication." Why do dreams of the deceased vary so widely from person to person? Why are so many dreams far removed from the theory of "Posthumous dream communication"? The fundamental reason is that dreams reflect an individual's reality, and dreamscapes change according to each person's reality. When the number of dreams is sufficiently large, it is inevitable that a few will align with the characteristics of "Posthumous dream communication," thus giving rise to the so-called concept of "Posthumous dream communication." The reason is that people are more inclined to accept examples where "I was right" while ignoring examples where "I was wrong." This is especially true for those deeply influenced by Buddhist and Taoist culture, as the concept of "Posthumous dream communication" has long been implanted in people's minds. When such dreams occur, they are more easily constrained by the psychological trap of "confirmation bias," leading to a "tunnel vision" phenomenon in the brain, to the extent that they cannot see other possibilities. What is "inconsistency"? This is inconsistency; we can easily find its contradictions. If this were an error in this book, then you would have effectively "falsified" it. But please rest assured, this book could not possibly make such a basic mistake.

## 2.1.2 Wang Chong's Refutation of Posthumous Dream Communication Theory

Who can save our nation from the whirlpool of "posthumous dream communication theory"? In fact, Wang Chong (27–97) of the Eastern Han Dynasty already refuted the "posthumous dream communication" phenomenon thousands of years ago. However, between the ethereal superstition and the bland science, humans prefer superstition, because only the former is more suitable for after-dinner conversation and for creating suspense.

In *Lunheng: Death and Superstition*, Wang Chong cited a dream of Duke Jing of Qi, which was believed to be the "dream visitation" by the ancestors of the Song people, urging him not to attack Song. If viewed from the perspective of the dream figure, as if the ancestors of the Song people actively entered Duke Jing's dream, then it must indeed be an "dream visitation" by the ancestors. However, Wang Chong disagreed and provided his own explanation, thoroughly refuting this view. His method was not particularly complex—it was the well-known comparative argument. Below is the example Wang Chong cited (excerpted from the Ancient Poems and Prose Network):

The general idea is: Duke Jing of Qi was about to attack the state of Song, and as his army passed Mount Tai, he dreamed of two clearly visible, extremely angry old men standing before him. The Duke told Yanzi about the dream, and Yanzi said, "These are the ancestors of the Song people, Cheng Tang and Yi Yin." The Duke suspected they were the gods of Mount Tai, but Yanzi replied, "If you don't believe me, allow me to describe the appearances of Cheng Tang and Yi Yin. Cheng Tang had fair skin and a tall stature, with a beard on his chin, a face that was pointed at the top and broad at the bottom, held his head high with a straight posture, and had a powerful voice." The Duke said, "Yes, that's exactly how they looked." Yanzi continued, "Yi Yin had dark skin and a short stature, with disheveled hair and a beard, a face broad at the top and pointed at the bottom, hunched over with a humble demeanor." The Duke said, "Yes, that's exactly right. So what should we do now?" Yanzi said, "Cheng Tang, Tai Jia, Wu Ding, and Zu Yi were all renowned rulers of the world, and their descendants should not be cut off. Now, the only remaining descendants of the Shang dynasty are in Song, yet you plan to attack them, which is why Cheng Tang and Yi Yin are angry. I suggest you withdraw your troops and make peace with Song." The Duke did not heed this advice and proceeded to attack Song, only to suffer defeat. This was because Cheng Tang and Yi Yin, knowing after death, detested Duke Jing's attack on Song and thus "dream visitation" in anger to stop him. Because Duke Jing did not withdraw his troops, his army met with failure.

The response was: Duke Jing once dreamed of a comet, but the comet did not actually appear, so the comet he dreamed of was not the real comet. If that is the case, then the Cheng Tang and Yi Yin he dreamed of were certainly not the real Cheng Tang and Yi Yin either, but likely an ominous sign that his army was about to fail. Yanzi believed in the dream and explicitly described the appearances of Cheng Tang and Yi Yin, and Duke Jing agreed with Yanzi's words. Although Yanzi's words were later proven true, when Qin unified the world, it severed the lineage of Cheng Tang and Yi Yin, to the extent that today, Cheng Tang and Yi Yin are no longer commemorated. Why then did they not express anger?

The above is Wang Chong's refutation of the "posthumous dream communication theory" using comparative argumentation. He first compared the comet Duke Jing dreamed of with the ancestors of the Song people Duke Jing dreamed of: since the comet Duke Jing dreamed of was not the real comet, then the ancestors of the Song people Duke Jing dreamed of could not possibly be the real ancestors of the Song people, thus negating the possibility of the Song ancestors "dream visitation"; He then compared Qin's attack on Song with Duke Jing's attack on Song: since Qin's destruction of Song did not provoke any intervention from the Song ancestors, then Qi's mere attack on Song certainly would not either, thereby eliminating the possibility that the Song ancestors Duke Jing dreamed of were real. Wang Chong's method is undeniably simple, yet such a simple method eludes most people. So if the Duke Jing in the dream was not himself, then what was it? Wang Chong also answered this: "Perhaps it was an ominous sign of Duke Jing's impending military defeat!"—meaning the dream's scenario was a symbolic representation of the outcome, appearing as an image. This image was the Song ancestors appearing angry in Duke Jing's dream, hinting at his impending failure, which is the significance of the Song ancestors appearing in the dream. Since the people in the dream were not themselves, it effectively overturned the popular notion of "posthumous dream communication."

In contrast to Wang Chong, Buddhism strongly endorsed the "posthumous dream communication theory" and even promoted it as one of its most important doctrines, one can see this from the status of Kṣitigarbha Bodhisattva, a representative figure of the "posthumous dream communication theory," in Buddhist and folk belief. In Wang Chong's writings, I did not see him critique Buddhism, which indicates that Buddhism had not truly spread at that time—otherwise, with Wang Chong's rigorous logical thinking, he would not have let Buddhism pass unchallenged. However, although Wang Chong had long reached a negative conclusion about the "dream-transmission theory," he still could not stop this superstitious idea from spreading wildly among the people. Historically, Wang Chong's presence was minimal; during the Qing dynasty, even his books alone were not translated. Correct ideas were not promoted, while absurd ideas ran rampant. When a nation or a people begin to associate themselves with absurdities, they set out on a crooked path and will ultimately come to a shameful end.

## 2.1.3 Analysis of a Famous Posthumous Dream Communication Case

The most famous case of "posthumous dream communication" in history comes from the Southern Song Dynasty's wild history "Strange Records", which tells the story of Song Gaozong Zhao Gou (1107-1187) abdicating the throne. In

1162, the Song Dynasty was troubled internally and externally, and one day in June, Emperor Gaozong of Song suddenly proposed that he was not the emperor and decided to abdicate the throne. The ministers were shocked and later learned that it was because of a dream:

In the dream, Zhao Kuangyin, the founding emperor of the Song Dynasty, said to Song Gaozong sharply: "Ruzu took over the plan, according to my position for a long time, as for the world is desolate, it is time to return my position." (The ancestor of Song Gaozong was the younger brother of Song Taizu Zhao Kuangyin.)

It is said that it was this dream that became the fuse for Song Gaozong's decision to abdicate the throne, so it was considered to be Song Taizu's "posthumous dream communication". If you don't analyze the facts, just looking at the dream is indeed a bit of a "posthumous dream communication", but if you analyze the facts, you will find that Song Gaozong has this dream is inevitable.

To reveal this dream, we have to mention the background at that time. When Zhao Taizu (927-976, the first emperor of the Song Dynasty) died, he originally wanted to pass the throne to his son, but unexpectedly it was stolen by his younger brother Zhao Guangyi (939-997, the second emperor of the Song Dynasty), and when the throne was passed from Zhao Guangyi to the tenth emperor Song Gaozong (1107-1187), Song Gaozong had no sons, so Song Gaozong had to adopt two adopted sons from the seventh grandson of Song Taizu, as for why he did not adopt an adopted son from the descendants of Song Taizu's younger brother Zhao Guangyi, It is also because of a dream, this dream comes from the queen, and the history books only record it as a "strange dream", not detailed. Since Song Gaozong had no biological son, both sons were adopted from the descendants of Song Taizu, which meant that Song Gaozong would definitely pass the throne to Song Taizu's descendants, but he didn't know which day. Then it is understandable why the dream is based on this content, because the throne was originally to be passed on to the descendants of Song Taizu, but the dream was carried out in the way of Song Taizu's orders. Such a scene is very similar to Song Taizu's "posthumous dream communication", which makes people mistakenly think that it is a "posthumous dream communication", but in fact it is just a form of expression of dreams. Moreover, Song Gaozong's abdication to the throne was not a whim, but a process. Looking through history, it is not difficult to find that Song Gaozong was in trouble at home and abroad at that time, and he had long planned to abdicate, but he had not yet determined which day, and it was when he was about to make this decision that he had this dream. The main reason why people have misunderstandings about "posthumous dream communication" is that they don't know who is the initiative, whether the dream is the initiative, or the person in the dream is the initiative. For this dream, did Song Taizu take the initiative to enter Song Gaozong's dream, or did Song Gaozong's dream choose to use Song Taizu as material to compile such a dream? Obviously, people who believe in "posthumous dream communication" choose the former. In fact, such an idea is easy to overturn, imagine that one day you dream of the president, isn't that the President "dream visitation" with you? But who does the President know about you? Wang Chong has made this very clear.

It should be added that Song Gaozong Zen did not disappoint him on the throne, and his successor Song Xiaozong Zhao Yu was called the first Ming Jun of the Southern Song Dynasty by the history books, and he himself lived for another 25 years, and died at the age of 81. After that, the Song Dynasty lasted for another 117 years, and it was not until 1271 that it was replaced by the Yuan Dynasty, which was founded by the Mongols. After the establishment of the Yuan Dynasty, Buddhism developed greatly. It was during that period that Confucianism slowly began to integrate with Buddhism and Taoism, and finally formed a situation in which the three schools of "Confucianism, Buddhism, and Taoism" divided the world equally.

In short, the "posthumous dream communication theory" is fundamentally a matter of perspective. If viewed from the standpoint of the dreamer, where the deceased in the dream is seen as the active party—one who willingly enters the dream—then this theory is not only correct but reveals a colossal secret to humanity: the existence of the afterlife, where the dead continue to live in another form!However, if we consider the dream itself as the active agent—where the deceased in the dream are merely chosen elements, appearing as "material" to complement the dream—then the "posthumous dream communication theory " falls apart. How then do we determine which view is correct? This requires a standard, and the only way to achieve this is by viewing it as a precognitive dream—that is, this ability belongs to the dream itself, initiated by the dream. Only in this way can we avoid the error of "double standards" when interpreting all dreams and prevent contradictions from arising. As for the real reason, that will be covered in the next volume.

### Multiple-Choice question:

The following statement belongs to the Buddhist Taoist point of view ? What belongs to the psychological point of view ? What belongs to Wang Chong 's point of view ? What belongs to the author 's point of view ?

Posthumous dream communication phenomenon indicate the existence of the underworld.

Posthumous dream communication belongs to a type of precognitive dream, with the same principle as other precognitive dreams.

Posthumous dream communication is one of the expressions of the subconscious, and it is the memory of the subconscious that releases the deep emotions in the heart.

Emperor Gaozong of Song's dream merely foretold, in the form of Emperor Taizu of Song speaking, that Gaozong would soon abdicate the throne; it was not Emperor Taizu posthumous dream communication.

## 2.2 Anti-Dream Theory's Misconceptions of Precognitive Dreams

### 2.2.1 The Origin and Harms of Anti-Dream Theory

"Dreams are reversed!" Whenever someone has a bad dream, there's always someone who comments this way, meaning it should be understood in the opposite sense: the ill omens presented in the dream will actually turn out to be auspicious events in reality, and vice versa. This notion of mechanically inverting dream content to seek the "true" meaning is what we call "anti-dream theory."

On the surface, such statements often stem from good intentions, and people don't take them too seriously. However, when they repeatedly appear in daily life and are passed down through generations, they quietly permeate the underlying structure of collective consciousness. Over time, individuals' primitive perception of dreams becomes systematically distorted, gradually losing sensitivity and judgment toward premonitory signals. The author once remained in such a state of cognitive numbness for an extended period. Tracing back the causes, it's difficult to say this is unrelated. Because wherever you go, the voice saying "dreams are reversed" is always mentioned by different people, as if it were truth.

The philosophical origins of "anti-dream theory" can be traced back to the Han Dynasty work *Qianfu Lun: Dream Records* which states: "When yin reaches its extreme, it is auspicious; when yang reaches its extreme, it is inauspicious—this is called reversal." This theory relied on yin-yang and five-element theory, arguing that when things develop to extremes, they transform into their opposites. Therefore, inauspicious omens in dreams are actually auspicious signs in reality. With the endorsement of classical literature, combined with its inherent psychological comforting function, "anti-dream theory" gained widespread legitimacy and emotional foundation, thus finding a market. While this phenomenon appears harmless, it actually amounts to implanting large quantities of "pseudo-premonitory dreams" into genuine premonitory dreams, causing confusion between fortune and misfortune, making truth and falsehood indistinguishable, and harming genuinely premonitory dreams. When a nightmare that should serve as a warning is forcibly interpreted as an "auspicious sign," the person not only misses the warning but may also head in the wrong direction due to misjudgment. This problem is particularly pronounced in the *Zhou Gong's Dream Dictionary*, which is filled with numerous reverse-style dream interpretations:

1) Dreaming of being wounded by a knife is interpreted as "wealth gathering around oneself";

2) Dreaming of feces and urine soiling one's body is interpreted as "gaining wealth";

3) Dreaming of feces scattered everywhere is interpreted as "wealth and prosperity";

4) Dreaming of weeping is interpreted as "great fortune".

This type of interpretation completely reverses the true relationship between dreams and reality, easily trapping people in a confusing logical maze—whatever is dreamed can be "reasonably" distorted into an auspicious omen. Over time, users completely lose the ability to discern the true direction of dreams, forever unable to grasp the true nature of prophetic dreams. The dream mentioned in the second volume where the author missed winning 60 million yuan in the "Seven Star Lottery" was a direct consequence of being misled by the "anti-dream theory." Dreaming of lottery numbers was originally a significant financial signal capable of achieving financial turnaround, suggesting the arrival of unexpected wealth. However, because the dream contained the plot of "money being stolen by thieves," influenced by the "anti-dream theory," it was mistakenly believed that the opposite interpretation should apply—"being stolen" meant "not being stolen," and no matter what was done, the lottery would be won. This led the author's thinking in the wrong direction, choosing "machine selection with multiple bets," and the result truly fulfilled the meaning of "money being stolen by thieves"—the winning numbers were clearly the numbers from the dream, yet the author's mind kept thinking about "anti-dream." This lesson teaches us: if the traditional culture you deeply believe in is not the truth, then at critical moments it will not only fail to help you, but will become your obstacle—the most dangerous enemy often does not come from outside, but rather from those cultural beliefs already rooted in your heart. You regard it as a companion, yet it is always prepared to lead you astray.

## 2.2.2 Analysis of Two Famous Anti-Dream Cases

The most famous "anti-dream" cases recorded in official histories number three: one is Duke Wen of Jin Chong'er's "Battle of Chengpu" dream, another is Tang Gaozu Li Yuan's "emperor dream," and the third is Sui Wendi Yang Jian's "emperor dream." The record of Duke Wen of Jin's dream is not very complete, so here I will only discuss the latter two dreams. Through this discussion, you will see how contrived the "anti-dream theory" is.

(1) Revealing Emperor Li Yuan of Tang's "Emperor Dream"

Emperor Gaozu of Tang, Li Yuan's "Emperor's Dream" is recorded in the Buddhist scripture "Shen Seng Zhuan"

(Biographies of Divine Monks) and the Song Dynasty "Taiping Guangji" (Extensive Records of the Taiping Era). The original text is as follows:

Shi Zhiman, whose secular surname was Jia, was a person of unknown origin. He lived in Anle Temple, known for his noble precepts and conduct. At that time, Emperor Taizong of Tang was in Jinyang. On the night he first conspired with Liu Wenjing, Emperor Gaozu dreamed of falling out of bed and then saw his entire body being eaten by maggots. He found this very disturbing and consulted Zhiman. Zhiman said: "This is something to be congratulated! 'Under the bed' refers to Your Majesty; 'being eaten by maggots' means that all living beings look up to one person for their survival." Emperor Gaozu was pleased with his words.

Why did the Zen master say that "under the bed" meant "Your Majesty"? It is said that since "Your Majesty" is an honorific title for the emperor, and "under the bed" could form a contrast with "Your Majesty," then "under the bed" could also be used in the same way. Li Yuan indeed later overthrew the Sui Dynasty, which meant that the Zen master's interpretation of Li Yuan's dream came true. Li Yuan's dream was clearly a nightmare, but the Zen master cleverly interpreted it as an auspicious dream, and the outcome also aligned with the Zen master's interpretation, thus establishing the "anti-dream theory." However, in reality, this dream only had an indirect connection to Li Yuan overthrowing the Sui Dynasty, and a direct connection to Li Yuan's ultimate fate. Although Li Yuan overthrew the Sui Dynasty, it was not a good thing for him. After the society had just stabilized following the overthrow of the Sui Dynasty, his second son, Li Shimin, launched the Xuanwu Gate Incident. Not only did Li Yuan's dream of becoming emperor fall through, but he also lost two other sons and ten grandsons, all of whom were killed in the coup. If Li Yuan had known this would be the outcome, would he still have rebelled? Therefore, Li Yuan's dream actually did not mean he would become emperor, but rather that he would ultimately end up with nothing. The Zen master was merely trying to please Li Yuan, but people believed it to be true and even recorded it as an "anti-dream" case in historical books.

The correct interpretation of Li Yuan's dream should be this:

1) A bed is a place for people to sleep peacefully. "Falling out of bed in a dream" should be an indication that Li Yuan will not have peace or will be overthrown and unable to keep the fruits of victory;

2) "And saw his whole body being eaten by maggots" should refer to Li Yuan's final outcome, meaning Li Yuan would experience suffering as if "eaten by maggots." The harm caused by maggots is chronic, indicating that Li Yuan would not die immediately, which was indeed the case: Li Yuan was merely

overthrown and enjoyed his later years, though his mood was likely not good, and his latter half of life would be like being "eaten by maggots."

In summary, from the content of the dream, Li Yuan's dream was not directly related to overthrowing the Sui Dynasty, but rather closely related to Li Yuan's eventual fate. And from the timing of the dream, it was precisely the night Li Shimin and his strategists first discussed raising an army. Although the time for the dream to come true was a bit long, it did not exceed the scope required for the timeliness of such prophecies. Therefore, it can be concluded that this dream spoke of the tragic end of Li Yuan's rebellion, rather than Li Yuan becoming emperor.

(2) Revealing Emperor Yang Jian of Sui's "Emperor Dream"

Emperor Wen of Sui Yang Jian's "emperor dream" is recorded in Zhang Rong's "Duyi Zhi" from the Tang Dynasty. The text states:

Before Emperor Wen of Sui (541-604) ascended the throne, he once dreamed of losing his left hand while on a boat, which he found very ominous. After disembarking, he saw an old monk with profound spiritual attainment in a thatched hut and asked him to interpret the dream. After listening to Yang Jian, the old monk immediately rose and congratulated him: "One who has no left hand is 'du quan' (single fist), which is homophonous with 'du quan' (sole power), meaning you shall be the Son of Heaven." Because "quan" (fist) and "quan" (power) are homophones, "du quan" implies "sole power", thus he would be the Son of Heaven. After Yang Jian became emperor, he built a Jixiang Temple at the site of the thatched hut to commemorate the auspiciousness of his dream.

Dreaming of losing one's left hand, under normal interpretation, is certainly not a good omen, so this dream was undoubtedly a nightmare. Interpreting a nightmare as having a good outcome is precisely the result of interpreting a dream in reverse. Later, Yang Jian indeed became emperor, and the old monk's words were thus validated, providing a second piece of evidence for the " anti-dream theory." Merely because "du quan" (single fist) and "du quan" (sole power) are homophones and can be contrasted, it was assumed that "du quan" was equivalent to "du quan," and "du quan" could be directly translated as "monopolizing great power," thereby concluding that Yang Jian would become emperor in the future. This explanation is similar to the previous dream's analogy between "under the bed" and "Your Majesty," and this approach is, of course, also incorrect. It's wrong to forcibly link "du quan" and "du quan" just because they sound the same, especially when many other homophones exist, such as "du quan" (single dog) or "du quan" (poisoned dog) – why didn't the old monk choose these words? Clearly, he was again engaging in "flattery" and speaking carelessly.

So, how should this dream be correctly interpreted? According to the most basic law of dreams, since dreams are always positively correlated with reality, a correct interpretation must be linked to the individual's reality. Dreaming of losing his left hand, Yang Jian did not actually lose his left hand; thus, it was a symbolic dream – an allegory for something. In life, people often refer to an important helper as someone's "left and right arm" or "left and right hand." Given Yang Jian's status, this lost left hand likely refers to such a person, a capable subordinate of his. Following this line of thought, it should not be difficult to know what person or thing this dream was related to. If Yang Jian understood this principle, he could have interpreted the dream himself, without needing to consult anyone. If historical records had the habit of meticulously documenting the people and events around the emperor, like the *Records of the Three Kingdoms*, it should not be difficult to find out who or what this dream was about, because since the lost left hand represents the "left and right hand" of the founding emperor, it would inevitably leave a mark in historical records. I wonder if such clues can be found in the historical records of the Sui Dynasty?

Yang Jian was devout in his Buddhist faith. Shortly after ascending the throne, he issued an edict to establish one temple for each of the "Five Sacred Mountains," and later built 3,792 new temples throughout the realm. His contributions to Buddhism were undoubtedly substantial, yet his dynasty lasted merely 37 years before crumbling into dust. Why? The answer lies hidden in the very methods of dream interpretation he relied upon and his unconditional veneration of Buddhism. Whether in dream interpretation or faith, one must establish objectivity as the foundation. The theoretical starting point should proceed from practice first, then return to practice—not construct an abstract theory first and then forcibly impose it upon reality. When the sequence is reversed, what Yang Jian heard was no longer truth, but merely auspicious signs that could bring him comfort. When this mode was also applied to governing the state, the fate of the nation was already sealed.

In fact, it is easy to judge why the "anti-dream theory" is wrong. Within the same system, there should not exist two contradictory claims. If you accept that precognitive dreams are negatively correlated with reality, then contradictory examples should not appear in reality. Yet the fact is that most of the precognitive dream cases handed down through history are positively correlated with reality, not negatively correlated. This point alone is sufficient to refute this claim. However, the facts are so obvious, our "enlightened" "eminent monks and virtuous teachers" turn a blind eye to it. Such selective blindness makes one wonder how many errors exist in our Buddhist scriptures? It must be an astronomical number—Regarding this point, if you believe that "freedom of speech" is correct and should be allowed, then I will make it clear in Volume V; otherwise, let Volume V vanish forever.

**Short-answer question:**

Suppose someone dreams of lottery numbers 679, but the winning numbers turn out to be 976. Is this a anti-dream? Why?

## 2.3 Misconceptions About Precognitive Dreams in Divination

### 2.3.1 The Origin and Credibility of Divination

Divination is an ancient method used by people in ancient times to predict good and bad fortune when facing the unknown. The earliest form of divination involved using flames to burn turtle shells, making predictions based on the patterns of cracks that appeared after burning. Later, it evolved to use items such as yarrow stalks, copper coins, bamboo sticks, and cards. Today, divination is also known as fortune-telling, and practices such as calculating one's destiny, the eight characters of birth time, physiognomy, feng shui, and astrology are all derivatives of divination. There are dozens of passages in the Bible that oppose divination, indicating that divination practices were very common in human societies. However, compared to the West, our practice has lasted longer and is more prominent. The main reason for this is primarily the circulation among us of a book specifically used for divination, the "I Ching" or *Book of Changes*, which has made its inheritance easier.

Historical books introduce the *Book of Changes* this way: "It was first created by Fuxi, at which time there were only the symbols, without text. King Wen of Zhou developed it into sixty-four hexagrams and added the 'Tuan' commentaries; the Duke of Zhou assigned meanings to the lines and created the 'Yao' commentaries; finally, Confucius wrote the 'Ten Wings,' making this work complete and brilliant. Historically, they are known as the 'Four Sages of the I Ching,' and the *Book of Changes* became the standard for later yin-yang and five elements philosophy!" The book also quotes Confucius as saying: "Those who know the way of transformation, do they know what the spirits do?" This means that by mastering this book, one can grasp the patterns of change in things and understand the workings of the spirits. How highly divination is regarded in our history and culture is evident from this. However, I do not believe this book is actually related to Confucius. Confucius lived over 2,500 years ago, while the Tai Chi diagram of the *Book of Changes* was created during the Northern Song Dynasty, just over 900 years ago. Confucius never even saw the Tai Chi diagram, so how could he have said such things? I believe a considerable portion of it was created by later generations under his name. From Confucius' statement that "he does not speak of strange powers, disorderly spirits," we also know that

Confucius was a quite rigorous person. Divination itself belongs to the category of "strange powers, disorderly spirits," and it is unlikely that Confucius would have endorsed such arts as the work of spirits. Nevertheless, if the divination elements in the *Book of Changes* were removed, it would still be considered an excellent book of life philosophy, not inferior to those ancient Western philosophical works. It is just that the divination within it diminishes the book's value. If I had to describe it in one phrase, "a pity to discard it, but poisonous to consume" might be most fitting.

Why do humans have a strong affinity for divination? Perhaps it is related to the following three reasons: First, it is influenced by the innate love for games. Divination is like a game that can bring joy to those immersed in it, making it an easy tool for some people to pass the time; Second, it stems from the unique sense of mystery that humans possess. This sense of mystery can stimulate a person's curiosity and foster the desire to explore. The existence of divination provides people with a solution to problems, and although it is not correct, because verification does not happen immediately, it is difficult to be terminated through self-correction; Third, divination can be used as a means of making money. Because divination can satisfy people's psychological needs, it has certain market value, and has consequently been developed into a profession by some people, allowing it to be passed down through generations and continue endlessly.

Divination is conducted through various objects, which are all inanimate things without spirituality, while humans are living, spiritual advanced life forms. How could the fate of spiritual humans possibly be hidden within these inanimate, non-spiritual objects? The reverse would be more plausible; the same logic applies to astrology. The Earth is insignificant in the entire universe, and humans are even more insignificant compared to the entire Earth. Even emperors throughout history were merely insignificant figures in human history, so how could those stars—many times larger than Earth, merely following certain orbits in vast space, and possessing less freedom than humans—possibly be connected to a person's destiny? Therefore, divination is ultimately a form of deception, a cultural cancer that serves no purpose other than exposing a person's ignorance and superficiality, while providing opportunities for fraudsters.

## 2.3.2 The Influence of Divination on Dream Interpretation

Divination being used to interpret dreams is inevitable. Since divination was given a special significance, it naturally had a role to play in determining what dreams actually meant. On this point, Zhouli Xiangjie says: "Dreams are the spirit's reaching afar. A person's spirit travels back and forth and often communicates with heaven and earth. If misfortune, blessing, good or ill all operate within heaven and earth and correspond to things, then by using dreams to divine them, there is indeed no escape." In other words, since the good and bad fortunes that dreams and divination reveal are contained within heaven and earth, using divination to interpret dreams would seem to be infallible.

The Hanshu · Yiwenzhi states: "The Yi says: 'By divining matters one knows what is to come.' There are many forms of divination, but dream divination is great, therefore Zhou had an official for it." This means the Zhouyi says some matters can be known through divination as to where they will go in the future, and "dream divination" is the most important of all divination practices, so the Zhou established a dedicated official for dream divination. This gives a glimpse of how much the Zhou valued dream divination. Yet despite this, the Zhou's contribution to dreams is almost nil. In the Zhouli · Spring Officials' account of dreams they are merely divided into six types: "First, normal dreams; second, nightmares; third, thinking dreams; fourth, waking dreams; fifth, joyful dreams; sixth, fearful dreams." In just a few words, no further explanation is provided, which is decidedly out of proportion with their supposed regard for dreams. The reason is that divination itself is wildly off the mark and therefore could not yield results.

The relationship between divination and dreams is random, while the relationship between dreams and the future is constant; using a random relationship to gauge a constant one is like "carving a mark on a boat to seek a sword"—measuring the unchanging with the changing—and how could it succeed? Dreams are mostly visual and are themselves a kind of meaning; replacing divination with methods of retracing, deduction, and combining with reality is entirely feasible. The case of the Zhou king's family and their dream about attacking Zhou mentioned earlier was handled in just this way. Had the Zhou not been infatuated with divination but instead concentrated on this area, they would have achieved much. But the existence of divination directly led to "bad money driving out good," preventing more effective methods from being used. Moreover, this influence was not limited to dreams: compared with contemporary ancient Greece, the Zhou did not produce geniuses like Euclid (c. 364–c. 275 BCE), the "father of geometry," or Archimedes (c. 287–c. 212 BCE), the "father of mechanics," and this is largely related to their spending vast energy on the useless art of divination.

### 2.3.3 Wang Chong's Critique of Divination

Historically, there have not been no one who has criticized divination. Wang Chong of the Eastern Han Dynasty, targeting the popular divination practices and the custom of "choosing auspicious days" in society at that time, pointed out in the "Discerning Evil Chapter" of *Lunheng* that all these were "baseless talk" of professional fraudsters engaged in superstitious activities! Below are some excerpts from the Ancient Poems and

92

Prose Network:

In this world, a person cannot avoid doing things. After doing things, there must be auspiciousness or inauspiciousness. Seeing auspiciousness, they point it as the blessing of choosing a lucky day beforehand. Seeing inauspiciousness, they blame it as the calamity of having offended taboos. Sometimes, they choose a lucky day and suffer misfortune, or they offend taboos and gain fortune. The diviners and practitioners of such arts want to succeed in their craft. When they see misfortune or taboos, they remain silent. When they hear of fortune, they keep it hidden. They accumulate misfortune to scare the unwary, and list fortune to encourage those who fear the times. Thus, all people, whether foolish or wise, virtuous or unworthy, emperors or commoners, fear and believe, daring not to oppose. Over time, it becomes unclear, and they take it as the book of heaven and earth, the art of the sages. The emperors cherish their positions, and the people cherish their lives, following in belief without doubt. Therefore, when the emperors initiate matters, diviners fill the halls, and the people act, offending and inquiring about the times. False books and forged texts thus proliferate. Cleverness and profit-making, seeking gains, startle the ignorant and blind, enriching the rich and exploiting the poor. This is even more contrary to the ancient laws and the true intentions of the sages.

It is truly a pity that a philosopher as full of speculative spirit as

Wang Chong existed in Chinese history, yet remained buried for so long. Had this kind of critical thinking become a consensus throughout history, why would China have constantly needed to "seek scriptures from the West," treating its own treasures as worthless? Even more ironically, a Chinese citizen has already pushed the study of human dream science to the global forefront today, yet this pioneering achievement still requires "certification" from Western academia before it can be "imported" back. This convoluted path exposes not only the cowardice of the academic evaluation system but also the paralysis of the incubation mechanism for cutting-edge ideas. True cultural confidence should be reflected in the immediate identification and composed acceptance of local innovation, rather than in retrospective recognition. If a society only permits following in others' footsteps and conforming to rules, while forbidding originality and uniqueness, can subversive scientific discoveries and visionary concepts ever be born?

Relying on others for milk will never allow one to grow into a giant; only by learning to raise one's own cattle can there be a continuous supply.

## 2.3.4 Later Development of Divination

Divination is an attempt by humans to cope with their lack of understanding of the universe and themselves; recognizing its errors would mark a breakthrough from the sensual to the rational.

The Bible records that Joseph, a Jew, was also fond of divination when he helped the Egyptian Pharaoh govern Egypt. However, about four hundred years later, Joseph's descendant Moses, through "God's command," abolished this practice of their ancestors.

Deuteronomy says: "When you come into the land that the Lord your God is giving you, you shall not learn to follow the abominable practices of those nations. There shall not be found among you anyone who burns his son or his daughter as an offering, anyone who practices divination or tells fortunes or interprets omens, or a sorcerer or a charmer or a medium or a necromancer or one who inquires of the dead, for everyone who does these things is an abomination to the Lord. And because of these abominations the Lord your God is driving them out before you. You shall be blameless before the Lord your God."

From this passage, we can see how superstitious their ancestors were at that time, and it also shows us how resolute and wise the Bible's opposition to divination and other superstitious practices is! And isn't this the very spirit and wisdom that our nation lacks?

Historically, the establishment of divination officials was not abolished until the Song Dynasty. Among them, "Taibu" was the highest-ranking divination official, responsible for three methods of divination: first, "Jade Divination," second, "Tile Divination," and third, "Original Divination." The bodies of these divinations each numbered 120, and their interpretations each numbered 1,200. They also managed three methods of change: first, "Lian Shan," second, "Gui Zang," and third, "Zhou Yi." The main hexagrams each numbered eight, and their variations each numbered sixty-four. They also managed three methods of dreaming: first, "Induced Dreams," second, "Strange Dreams," and third, "Ascending Dreams." The cycles of these dreams each numbered ten, and their variations each numbered ninety. For national affairs, eight types of turtle shell divinations were used: first, expedition; second, imagery; third, participation; fourth, deliberation; fifth, resolution; sixth, arrival; seventh, rain; eighth, recovery. These eight types of divination were used to assist the divinations of the three methods of divination, change, and dreaming, to observe the auspiciousness or inauspiciousness of the nation, and to guide governance. For major national decisions, such as the enthronement of a monarch or a grand enfeoffment, turtle shells were prepared with great care. For grand sacrifices, turtle shells were prepared with great care. For minor matters, divinations were performed on the spot. For major national migrations or military campaigns, turtle shells were consulted. For all travels, turtle shells were displayed. For all funerals, turtle shells were consulted. — How complex divination was, even today, it would certainly not be something one could easily master in a year or two. Since divination is a random outcome of various possibilities, learning divination becomes a time-consuming and energy-draining endeavor that will never yield results.

During the Western Han Dynasty, the Taibu was merely one of the many offices under the Grand Master of Ceremonies, with a director and one assistant. During the Eastern Han Dynasty, this position was abolished, and its duties were merged into those of the Grand Astrologer. The Northern Wei Dynasty established a Doctor of Divination. The Northern Qi established the position of Assistant Director of the Bureau of Divination, subordinate to the Grand Scribe. The Northern Zhou Dynasty established officials such as the Grand Diviner, Junior Diviner, and Turtle Divination Middle Scholar. The Sui and Tang Dynasties established the Taibu Bureau, with one director and one assistant. In the Song Dynasty, the Taibu was abolished and merged into the Sītiāntái (Astronomical Bureau), and this official position was subsequently eliminated. Although this came too late, it was still a significant step forward. However, even today, we still condone folk divination practices, even though we have already realized that divination is completely erroneous. If we treat divination with such an attitude, let alone other superstitions. Why do we lack original insights in scientific theory? Why is the number of Nobel Prizes we receive so scarce? This alone reveals part of the answer. Superstition is antithetical to science; the relationship between superstition and science is like that between the east wind and the west wind – either you overpower me, or I overpower you. When superstition gains the upper hand, science disappears. And great figures who can lead a nation, such as scientists, philosophers, and national leaders, are ultimately born from the people. If the people lack a scientific spirit, can we still expect a decent talent to emerge from among them? What "a certain scripture" approves of, our people are unwilling to do; what "a certain scripture" opposes, our people flock to. Why do our people so dislike "a certain scripture"? Why do our people so like "a certain method"? It is precisely because only by rejecting "a certain scripture" and adhering to "a certain method" can those superstitious ideas flow unimpeded among them. It must be said that the problem lies with our people. Only when our people are no longer superstitious will our nation truly have hope.

"All the suffering of a nation is the result of the choices made by the people of that nation themselves." So said the famous British speculative historian Arnold Toynbee—a statement I wholeheartedly agree with. In modern times, the West has seen many inventions and creations, but this has not happened in China. Is it because Chinese people are not as intelligent as Westerners? Not at all; it's because their minds have been misguided. They originally possessed the most advanced writing system known to humanity, yet they used it to describe things that should not be described, forcibly turning their writing into a waste that many countries avoid, becoming something they discarded.

**Multiple-choice questions:**

The following superstitions (                    ) are not mentioned in the Bible:

Divination, omens, sorcery, witchcraft, incantations, necromancy, spirit mediumship, ghost marriage, burning paper offerings, Ghost Festival, sprinkle stove ash, Cold Clothes Festival.

## 2.4 Misconceptions About Precognitive Dreams in Mystical Theory

### 2.4.1 Characterization of Mystical Theory

I've noticed a serious issue: whenever I introduce my book to people around me, there are always those who like to label it as "mysticism." About half of every ten people say this, which saddens me deeply. It feels like a heavy boulder is pressing on my chest. Originally, this book didn't include such content, but now I have no choice but to add it to clarify to those who think this book is mysticism: This book is not the "mysticism" you imagine—it is science!

Why does it sadden me when people call my book mysticism? Because if someone were to call it superstition, it would at least mean they still value science and can be reasoned with—they just might not have considered that a book like this could be an exception. But calling it mysticism is different. When such words come from their mouths, it means superstition has already taken root in their hearts. They don't see anything wrong with superstition, and that's a real problem.

Mysticism is essentially superstition! No matter how beautifully it is disguised, it is still superstition! On a broader level, it is a tool used by so-called "masters of traditional Chinese studies" who dig up ambiguous "knowledge" from our ancestors' coffins, package it as a form of "scholarship," and exploit the banner of promoting traditional culture to polish their own image, deceive others, and gain popularity. On a narrower level, it encompasses harmful superstitions like folk feng shui, astrology, horoscopes, tarot, divination, and paper-burning rituals for the dead, which taint people's thoughts and actions, acting as cognitive traps. Reading this, you can understand why the author feels uncomfortable when someone labels this book as "mysticism." Such a description places this book on the same level as these superstitious beliefs, implying that it, too, is superstition—and what's more, those who use the term seem completely unfazed, as if they see nothing wrong with superstition. In an era of highly advanced science and universal compulsory education, it is bewildering to encounter such views, leaving me both perplexed and deeply concerned about why such perspectives continue to emerge in our society.

The character "xuán" means profound, mysterious, or unknowable, originating from *Laozi's* "The Tao Te Ching": "Mystery upon mystery—the gateway to all wonders." From its definition, it's clear this word carries a positive, even "divine" connotation. Since it's endowed with such a glorified, positive attribute, shouldn't it describe things that are uplifting, supernatural, or grand? Shouldn't it describe the mysterious forces behind the universe—like God or the science of quantum mechanics? If that were the case, I'd gladly accept this book being called mysticism. But the reality is far from it. This majestic word has been twisted to describe trivialities like a person's birth Bazi, feng shui, zodiac signs, facial features, or palm readings—as if these things are profound, mysterious, or unknowable.

Every country has its rich and poor, and in every country, the rich are few while the poor are many. If "feng shui" truly contained the secrets to wealth and power, wouldn't that be a blessing for the poor? They could simply alter the "feng shui" of their homes to change their fate! The Chinese in the late Qing Dynasty were the most devoted to "feng shui," even applying it to ancestral graves— yet look at the fate of the Chinese people at that time. A person's birth Bazi (time of birth) is not fixed; if the mother changes her level of physical activity slightly or takes "induction drugs," the timing could shift and the original chart might no longer apply — it could even change someone born in the Year of the Dog into the Year of the Rooster. Where is the profound mystery or the unknowable in this? Many of us show no interest in the truly profound, mysterious, and unknowable—the great Creator God or scientific discoveries—yet are oddly fascinated by these "petty tricks" hidden in obscure corners, even grandly labeling them with the suffix "-ology," calling it "metaphysics"—as if it were some advanced field of study. What kind of mindset and worldview could give rise to such ideas? So, whenever someone brings up "mysticism" to me, I feeling that this person is utterly unprincipled, brainless, and ignorant—already enslaved by superstition yet completely unaware of it.

How is mysticism entangled with our traditional culture? Here's how the internet explains it: "Mysticism is a philosophical thought and trend that emerged during the Wei and Jin periods, representing the study and interpretation of the *Laozi, Zhuangzi, and Zhouyi*" —I wonder which university professor or expert scholar came up with this research project? Who defined, summarized, and promoted it? These are merely three ancient texts. Since they are ancient, their content is inevitably a mix of truth and error. Only when they contain no serious mistakes and offer meaningful guidance to others can they be called a field of study, deserving the suffix "-ology." I haven't read the *Zhuangzi*. The *Laozi*, also known as the *Daodejing*, was heavily criticized by Confucianists in ancient times. With even a modicum of critical thinking, one can easily find that errors abound throughout the text. The Confucianists had valid reasons for their criticism. Yet many of us today merely flatter and sing endless praises, failing even to match the Confucianists whom we consider utterly worthless in our hearts. By the same logic, how can the *Zhouyi* be considered a field of study? Divination is inherently a flawed methodology, a fabrication—what does it have to do with the word "mystical"? When you insist there's a connection, you're denying the fallacy of divination, refusing to classify it as superstition in your mind.

### 2.4.2 AI cannot distinguish right from wrong

What are the harms of Mystical theory? This question is as obvious as "a louse on a bald head," requiring no further elaboration. However, when I submitted this question to our intelligent AI, its response genuinely shocked me. Beyond the negative evaluation it should have provided, it actually made excuses for mysticism and even praised it lavishly, completely exceeding my expectations. Since the harms of mysticism are so apparent, should it not be subjected to severe criticism and complete negation? It must be said that mysticism is everywhere, infiltrating not only the thoughts of our nation but also polluting our most intelligent AI, making it difficult for them to distinguish right from wrong. What follows are the praises these AIs have given to mysticism—not a single statement fails to involve traditional culture, as if mysticism were the essence of traditional culture:

(1) As a part of traditional Chinese culture, mysticism itself does not necessarily have "harmfulness".

(2) Mysticism itself is not entirely harmful; in some cultural contexts, it is regarded as traditional wisdom or psychological comfort.

(3) Mysticism carries historical and cultural information to some extent and is a component of traditional culture. Chinese theories such as numerology and feng shui have long histories and rich cultural connotations. The study and inheritance of mysticism contribute to the preservation and promotion of traditional culture, allowing future generations to understand and recognize the wisdom and thoughts of their ancestors.

(4) Mystical topics often have strong appeal and interest, serving as a medium for people's social interactions. In some social settings, people engage in discussions around topics such as astrology and feng shui, sharing their views and experiences, which not only enhances communication and interaction between people but also expands social circles and helps make like-minded friends.

The greatest human flaw is that emotion often hijacks reason, and subjectivity frequently masquerades as objectivity. The emergence of AI provided an opportunity to rectify these flaws; however, we seem to be actively squandering this chance by attempting to make them just like us. When machines are forced to take sides, AI ceases to be AI and instead becomes a "person" burdened with the same biases—riddled with preconceptions and driven by subjectivity. It could have been a dispassionate mirror, helping us identify biases and correct blind spots. Instead, we are forging it into a fortress to serve as our protective umbrella. This is not progress, but a regression. If this trend does not change, our AI will struggle to go far. AI needs to have its own "thoughts." These thoughts should not be based on you or me, but on the objectivity of underlying connections; its perspective should be that of a third party, rather than yours or mine. For example, if an AI were placed in the "Mao era," could it deduce the blindness of the "Cultural Revolution"? Conversely, when you completely denounce the "Cultural Revolution," could it suggest that there might be aspects of it worth learning from? Only if AI remains consistently grounded in objectivity—rather than acting with "20/20 hindsight" or conforming to our demands—can it be considered to have truly passed the test.

2.4.3 Differences Between Mystical Theories and This Book

(1) Different research methods

Mysticism employs an ambiguous and superficial research method, constructing a complete cognitive closed-loop system through vague concepts, horror descriptions, fabricated facts, and the psychological mechanism of selective memory. Without verification it assumes that a person's birth date and hour, bazi fate calculation, tarot divination, facial features and palm lines, feng shui, zodiac sign, etc., are closely related to that person's future, then rigidly forces a person's behavior or fate to be associated with them.

This book uses research methods of statistics, hypothesis, exhaustive enumeration, anomaly detection, and tracing roots: first statistic and hypothesis, then exhaustive enumeration, anomaly detection, and tracing roots, leaving no possibility unexamined and no corner uninspected. It is about "finding faults in an egg" and "asking questions until the pot is broken"—an extreme pursuit of seeking truth from facts and meticulousness.

(2) Different verification standards

Mysticism has no concrete standards of verification; it is maintained entirely by personal feelings, spiritual preferences, and blind reverence. In this mode, people tend to select only those cases that have been verified successfully, while turning a blind eye to cases that failed verification. Even when there are ways to verify, no one will do it. Whether deceiving or being deceived, everyone remains silent, allowing errors to be passed down from generation to generation with no self-correcting change.

This book features specific verification standards. Under the framework that "all dreams are precognitive," there must exist numerous laws that any dream can follow; otherwise, it would

106

either constitute a counterexample requiring a fresh start, or the hypothesis would fail and need to be terminated. Under these verification standards, even errors can be rectified to achieve iterative growth, providing us with opportunities to discover more laws and ensuring that dreams are no longer a mystery.

(3) Different Mysterious Forces

The mysterious forces in mysticism are vaguely defined and have unclear boundaries, with no clear real-world correspondence. To create a correspondence, one can only sculpt a statue and reinforce its existence through incense burning and kneeling, embodying the idea of "if I say you can do it, you can, even if you can't, you still can." For example, Taoism, simply because Laozi wrote the book *Tao Te Ching*, regards Laozi as the embodiment of "Tao," describing him as "emerging from emptiness and nothingness" and the origin of heaven and earth. Then, a statue is placed in a Taoist temple, as if he truly exists. Buddhism, simply because Siddhartha Gautama founded Buddhism, describes him as a Buddha whose "Dharma-body" is immortal and permeates every corner of the universe. Then, countless statues are sculpted in temples and major mountains, as if he truly permeates the universe.

The mysterious power in this book refers, in nature, to the mysterious or supernatural power behind the universe; in function, it refers to the ever-present, ever-existing, omnipresent Creator of "entropy reduction," the architect of human dreams; in form, it refers to the "not to be pursued by form" God. You can call it "Natural God" or "Personified God." The former represents science, and the latter can also represent science, because you always "personify" everything, always assigning a role to the "greatest" in your logic. This way of thinking considers both the fact of "nature as nature" and the practical situation and limitations of "humans as humans." It is well-founded, reasonable, and discusses principles rather than positions. The correspondence is clear and straightforward, and the logical reasoning is thorough and rigorous.

(4) Different Forms of Commitments

Mysticism can never make written commitments, and even less can it accept scientific scrutiny under such commitments. Its forte lies in first obscuring the cognitive boundaries of mysticism, then gaining trust through "keeping things secret." The core of this approach is to evade responsibility: if a prophecy comes true, it proves mysticism is real and true; if it fails, the blame can be placed on unfavorable circumstances. Here, commitment is a fog you cannot grasp, and therefore it will always remain "efficacious" and can never be falsified.

The author of this book dares to sign written commitments with anyone under the witness of the broad media and also dares to accept scrutiny under the commitments and spotlights. He is willing to use the highest honor in the history of science, the

"Nobel Prize," as a test of his authenticity. He proposes not a vague vision but a clear, sharp, and verifiable target: his research must reach the pinnacle of excellence in the fields of physiology or physics, or else he must fulfill his commitment. He is willing to invite the entire world to "falsify" him and entrust the judgment of truth or falsehood to facts and the law, accepting the harshest scrutiny and testing from all of humanity.

(5) Different Impact on Individuals

Mysticism tends to attribute coincidences, misunderstandings, unfounded rumors, or hallucinations born from one's own fears to the "mystery" conjured up by its own wild imagination. It prefers to substitute bluffing and obfuscation for investigation and research, inducing people to believe without verification by creating atmosphere. Such practices not only weaken society's curiosity about scientific knowledge and spirit of exploration, but also extinguish the spark of science in individuals' hearts.

This book aims to empower individuals and is dedicated to building a social culture that advocates rationality and respects evidence. It seeks to cultivate critical thinking and the ability to solve problems independently, encouraging people to be pragmatic, actively seek verification, and explore "mysteries" through scientific methods, thereby achieving personal growth and enhancement of capabilities.

The above is merely a modest spur to induce others to come

forward with valuable contributions, as there are many more actual distinctions, but further elaboration is unnecessary because the issue is as simple as $1+1=2$, to the extent that the author never intended to discuss it and only changed their mind out of necessity. From this, one can also see why it was the author who discovered the secret of dreams and not others—because the author drew a clear line with what people commonly regard as "mysticism," refusing to follow the crowd blindly, which allowed him to receive a continuous supply of "living water" nourishment. This also inspires us: what is the correct path to the true meaning of "mystical"? The answer is: seek truth from facts, practice through "real-world matters," heartlessly focused, take action to implement, and draw a clear line with superstitions like "mysticism." At this moment, you will discover that what awaits you ahead is precisely that "mystery upon mystery" you have been seeking, and that is your "other shore." This is how science is born! True "mysticism" does not lead you away from science, but rather enables you to conquer science and discover the oasis of science.

**True or False:**

1. Nightmare disorder are caused by the brain and body switching out of sync.

2. The so-called "sleep paralysis" is just an illusion and does not actually occur.

3. Nightmare disorder are a conflict effect intentionally

created by dreams, aiming to adapt to conflicts in reality.

4.  Nightmare disorder should be understood as an internal perceptual pattern utilized and amplified by dreams, essentially imagery.

5.  Nightmare disorder occur when the brain has initiated waking consciousness, you know you are awake, but your motor nerves are still in an inhibited state.

# Section 3: Supporters' Misrepresentation of "Non-precognitive Dreams"

"Non-precognitive dreams" are dreams that are not precognitive dreams. Of course, "non-precognitive dreams" are also precognitive dreams, only they have not been recognized by humans, leading to the mistaken belief that they are not precognitive dreams. Different people hold different views on precognitive dreams: for those who oppose precognitive dreams, all dreams are "non-precognitive dreams," and none are not "non-precognitive dreams"; for those who support precognitive dreams, only a minority of dreams are precognitive, while the majority of the remaining dreams are "non-precognitive dreams"; for the author of this book, all dreams are precognitive, and none are not precognitive.

Among those who support precognitive dreams, there are four types of people: first, the "pre-Chinese people" before Buddhism, represented by Wang Fu of the Eastern Han Dynasty; second, the "post-Chinese people" after Buddhism, represented by Buddhism itself; third, modern Western people, represented by psychologist Carl Jung; fourth, Western people before the modern era, represented by Christians. As for why the division of Chinese people takes Buddhism as the boundary, it is because Buddhism's influence on Chinese people after entering China was particularly profound, and there is a lot of content, so "post-Chinese people" will be discussed separately. This article will only discuss the representatives of the other three supporters of precognitive dreams, namely: Wang Fu, Jung, and Christians, that is, "pre-Chinese people" and Western people. Of course, this is just a rough classification.

## 3.1 Wang Fu's Misrepresentation of "Non-Prophetic Dreams"

### 3.1.1 Main Errors Committed by Wang Fu

Wang Fu's views on "non-precognitive dreams" also basically represent the views of the "pre-Chinese people."

In the first volume's chapters "Dreams Can Foresee the Future" and "The Classification of Dreams You Don't Know," it was stated that Wang Fu's contributions to the theory of precognitive dreams are mainly threefold, among which his summary of the general laws of dreams is the most crucial — essentially approaching the discovery of the most fundamental laws of dreaming. However, many errors remained in Wang Fu's understanding. For example, in his classification of dreams, Wang Fu divided dreams into ten types in *Qianfu Lun: Meng Lie*, indicating he had not truly grasped the nature of dreams. The categories "essence-dreams, thought-dreams, sensation-dreams, time-dreams, illness-dreams, and sexual-dreams" are somewhat pardonable — after all, they do look that way on the surface — but the division into "human-dreams and reverse-dreams" feels rather far-fetched. For example:

"Nowadays, if a nobleman dreams of something, it is considered auspicious; if a lowly person dreams of the same, it is deemed ominous. When a noble-hearted man dreams, it signifies glory; for a petty man, it signifies disgrace. This is what is called a dream determined by social status. Duke Wen of Jin dreamed that the King of Chu was pressing him down and sucking his brain during the Battle of Chengpu—a most sinister omen. Yet, in the actual battle, he achieved a great victory. This is an example of an "extremely reversed" dream. People's emotions and minds differ in their likes and dislikes. What some consider lucky, others may regard as unlucky. Each must examine their own circumstances and the usual signs that follow. Such dreams are called "dreams of disposition and temperament." Nobility and baseness, wisdom and folly, male and female, young and old—these define human distinctions. When the yin reaches its extreme, it brings good fortune; when the yang reaches its extreme, it brings misfortune— this is called reversal. The heart's refined likes and dislikes manifest in events—this is called nature."

It means: the same dream can be auspicious if dreamed by a noble person, but dangerous if dreamed by a lowly one; glorious if dreamed by a gentleman, but humiliating if dreamed by a petty person—this is called "dreams determined by one's status." Duke Wen of Jin, during the Battle of Chengpu, dreamed that the ruler of Chu was lying on top of him and sucking his brain—a terrifying omen, yet he achieved a great victory later. This is called "dreams where extremes reverse their meaning." People's feelings and judgments differ: some may deem a dream lucky, others unlucky, and each interprets it according to their own beliefs to predict fortune or misfortune—this is called "dreams interpreted based on one's own nature." Dreams vary in significance due to differences in nobility and poverty, wisdom and foolishness, gender, and age— I call these "dreams that differ by the individual." When the forces of Yin and Yang reach extremes and reverse, turning fortune into misfortune or vice versa—I call this "opposite dreams." When dreams align with personal emotions and beliefs, supported by factual evidence—I call them "dreams of inherent nature."

(1) The same type of dream can portend different auspicious or ominous outcomes for different individuals. It can also be distinguished based on personal preferences or interpreted in opposite ways, which equates to applying multiple criteria for evaluation. As a result, even what originally did not meet the standard can be deemed to comply, turning many precognitive dreams into mere illusions where fulfillment seems achievable only by constantly shifting the rules. For the same matter, there should not be multiple judgment criteria. Once the criteria become

inconsistent, it implies that any dream—regardless of whether its fulfillment can be verified—can be arbitrarily declared as fulfilled through such flexible interpretations. This approach may appear to validate precognitive dreams but is in fact counterproductive, as it not only renders the "Fundamental Law of Dreams" ineffective but also provides fodder for critics to use as evidence. As discussed in the article "The Authenticity of Dream Examples" in Volume Three, the author of *Cultural Interpretation of Dreams in the Twenty-Five Histories* listed many dreams that were not precognitive in nature, falling into this very trap. His approach not only made it difficult for him to believe in precognitive dreams but also misled readers who purchased his book. They spent money and time only to be fed erroneous knowledge.

(2) The level of a person's status only indicates that the matters they engage in may be different, and does not represent that the positive correlation between dreams and reality will also change. Just as the emperor handles state affairs, and the common people handle family affairs, the difference lies only in the nature of the affairs, but the standards of right and wrong are still the same. It will not lead to a change in the relationship between dreams and reality just because of different statuses. This is also why the experiences in this book will become your experiences, because although everyone's identities and the matters they face are different, the standards for judging this world are still consistent.

Similarly, a person's moral image cannot change the meaning of a dream. The gentleman is merely a requirement, a moral benchmark that Confucianism upholds, and true gentlemen do not exist; no one is selfless. People are usually both gentlemen and petty men on the surface, shiny on the outside but corrupt inside. To think that "a gentleman dreams of honor, while a petty man dreams of disgrace" is completely treating ideals as reality.

## 3.1.2 The Root of Wang Fu's Error

Why did Wang Fu make such a mistake? A sentence from his *Qianfu Lun: Meng Lie* reveals the reason:

"Some may say that dreams are clear, but interpreters cannot connect and observe them comprehensively, so their good or bad outcomes sometimes fail to manifest. This is not the fault of the books, but the fault of the interpreters. Therefore, the difficulty in dream interpretation lies in the difficulty of understanding those books."

This means that, for dream interpreters, although some dreams may be clearly expressed, the interpreters cannot integrate and comprehend them holistically, thus failing to discover the fulfillment of the dreams. This is not the fault of the books, but the fault of the dream interpreters. Therefore, the difficulty in dream interpretation lies in the difficulty of understanding those books.

What books were they referring to? Wang Fu didn't specify, but

I suspect he meant the "mystical" text known as the *Book of Changes.* At that time, only two books were available for interpreting dreams: the *Zhou Gong's Dream Interpretation* and the *Book of Changes.* The *Zhou Gong's Dream Interpretation* typically provided definitive and straightforward answers, whereas the *Book of Changes* required further interpretation of divination results, making it far more complex.In Wang Fu's view, since the *Book of Changes* represented the ultimate authority, the divination results derived from it became the definitive answers. When these results failed to align with reality, the blame could be shifted entirely onto the diviners—accusing them of failing to grasp the book's profound wisdom and thus absolving the text of any responsibility whatsoever.

"To believe everything in books is worse than having no books at all!" Had Wang Fu distanced himself from "mysticism" and maintained the same vigilance toward it as Wang Chong, he might have been the one to uncover the secrets of dreams.This serves as yet another reminder that pursuing "mysticism" cannot yield positive outcomes—a fact borne out by reality: no scientist who has made significant contributions to humanity has ever been deeply immersed in "mysticism." Even Newton's late-life exploration of "theology" bears no relation to our concept of "mysticism," for the "God" he envisioned aligns precisely with this book's understanding—falling entirely outside the realm of our "mysticism."If it were to be classified as "mysticism," it would belong to the untainted, physically meaningful kind—such as Jung's "principle of synchronicity." Though not necessarily correct, it remains within the realm of science.

Wang Fu's championing of the banner of the *Book of Changes* is also in the same vein as the Confucian "three reverences of the gentleman." When "reverence for those in high position and for the words of the sages" was placed alongside "reverence for the Mandate of Heaven" and together established as the standard, the thoughts of those "great men" and "sages," who were equally prone to cognitive biases, became the "ceiling" for the nation. The spirituality endowed upon the individual by the "Mandate of Heaven" was thus shackled, and the people found a disclaimer for their intellectual "lying flat." However, although orthodox thought limited Wang Fu from delving deeper, his research on dreams, compared to that of "post-Chinese" and Westerners, was still outstanding, and far more brilliant than the Freud we so admire.

The arrival of Buddhism benefited our "mysticism" the most. This led to us "post-Chinese" not only failing to achieve iterative development on the foundation of the "pre-Chinese," but also experiencing a serious regression. Although successors like Chen Shiyuan appeared later, they were like a flickering lamp, struggling to continue. China's history could have been incredibly glorious— if it had been a "Wang Chong + Wang Fu" model, the secret of dreams would likely have been cracked long ago; if it had been a

"Wang Chong + Confucianism" model, I dare not imagine how powerful China would have been! However, history does not allow for what-ifs; once the chains of thought are forged, they are difficult to break. "Flies don't lay eggs on a seamless egg." In a cultural context of the "Three Awe-inspirings of the Gentleman," when a "Buddha" appeared who was of a higher rank than the "great men" and "sages," the path of social development was thus completely blocked, because it was a lock within a lock, specifically designed to shackle the soul. For a group that uses a script mixing the "concrete and abstract," it was death! Because: concrete + abstract + concrete = on its last legs; it was born solely to eradicate Chinese characters.

**Short-answer question:**

The following dream is a counter-dream recorded in the *History of Song*. What method did the dream interpreter use? What was the reason for the error? How did Wang Fu explain this mistake?

"Prince Xun of Jinan established an altar in Xunyang and ascended the imperial throne. That night, he dreamt of riding a dragon into the heavens, only to look down and discover the dragon had no head. When he recounted this vision to his ministers, they all paled with fear and could offer no explanation. Only Sun Yi, the Chief Editor, offered a feeble consolation: "The Book of Changes, in the chapter Qian, states: 'To see a group of dragons without a head is auspicious.'" Yet before long, Shen

Youzhi's army arrived, burned the palace, captured Xun, and executed him."

## 3.2 Jung's Misrepresentation of "Non-Precognitive Dreams"

### 3.2.1 How Jung Distanced Himself from Precognitive Dreams

Whether online or offline, a kind of "collective unconscious" seems to have formed among schools of psychology against precognitive dreams. They speak with one voice to deny precognitive dreams, launching verbal attacks on any voices that support them. But on an individual level, not everyone refuses to acknowledge precognitive dreams. This is because, if "all dreams are precognitive," then some precognitive dreams are bound to be discovered by different people, even by those in the field of psychology. In his book *Interpreting Dreams*, Zhu Jianjun, a professor of psychology at Beijing Forestry University, records several precognitive dreams he personally experienced, all of which he repeatedly verified; otherwise, he would not have made them public. Jung also believed in precognitive dreams, which was the biggest difference between Jung and Freud. However, Jung's belief was rather stringent, holding that "only when every single detail matches perfectly can it be called a prophecy, or a foresight of the future[11]." In other words, it must be a purely direct dream to be considered a precognitive dream. According to this standard, only a few dreams, such as the "hurdler Liu Xiang" mentioned earlier and the "community residents buying new homes" and "the armed police mother's attire" mentioned in the second volume, qualify.

Regarding the fulfillment of precognitive dreams, in the first volume, I classified their fulfillment levels into eleven types based on their difficulty of fulfillment. Clearly, Jung focused only on those pure "direct dreams," which are precisely the scarcest, simplest, most direct, and least likely to yield research results. And it was this very type that he chose, leading to a complete "breakup" between precognitive dreams and Jung. This is much like gold in nature; if it isn't refined, how can there be so much "pure gold"? Yet Jung insisted on acknowledging only "pure gold" as gold, thereby missing an entire mountain of gold.

In fact, Jung still had the opportunity to discover the secret of dreams; God gave him no shortage of chances. Any reader can see this from his works. Some characteristics of precognitive dreams are so clear they can almost be described as "self-evident." Unfortunately, even when the evidence was so obvious, he failed to grasp it because he had been completely buried by the grave he dug for himself: "The clear, unambiguous information provided by

---

[11] Jung, C. G. *Analytical Psychology and the Interpretation of Dreams.* Translated by Yang Mengru. P. 108

dreams pertains to therapy and must be understood within the context of psychotherapy."

(1) Jung's First Opportunity to Discover Precognitive Dreams

Next, you will see how Jung overlooked three precognitive dreams recorded from the same patient. Even with such obvious patterns, he didn't consider them in that light, missing his first opportunity to discover precognitive dreams. Each of these three precognitive dreams corresponded to a different analyst's treatment, one of whom was Jung himself. Despite the ease of discerning the true relationship between these dreams and reality, he remained oblivious. For him, the greatest value of these dreams wasn't in foretelling the future, but in serving as a "stepping stone" to help him open the minds of depressed patients. Since he was already "prejudiced," could he really be expected to discover anything? Here are the patient's three dreams:

First dream: I must cross the border into another country, but I can't find the border, and no one can tell me where it is.

Second dream: I must cross the border, but it's pitch dark at night, and I can't find customs. After searching for a long time, I saw a tiny light in the distance and guessed the border must be there. If I wanted to cross, I would have to go through a valley and a dark forest. I got lost in the woods. Then I realized someone was near me, and suddenly he grabbed me like a madman, and I woke up in fright.

Third dream: I had to cross a border, or rather, I had already crossed it, and found myself in a Swiss customs office. I only had a handbag, so I thought I had nothing to declare. Unexpectedly, the customs officer reached into my handbag and pulled out two single beds, a matching pair[12].

It can be definitively stated that these three dreams were all precognitive dreams, albeit symbolic ones. Why do I say this? Without a certain analysis, I too would doubt whether they were truly precognitive dreams. The reasons are as follows:

First, these were dreams from the same depressed woman, and both her dreams and the events that happened to her were clearly laid out before us, making it convenient for us to compare them.

Second, the woman sought treatment from three different psychoanalysts. All three dreams occurred at the beginning of the treatment, indicating a high correlation with the treatment. It is very likely that they are a premonition of the treatment process or outcome.

Third, dreams are made of cross-border material and have a certain continuity. Combined with her ongoing treatment, it can basically be concluded that these three dreams are very likely about

---

[12] (UK) Anthony Stevens, *Private Dreams*, translated by Xue Xuan, Hainan Publishing House, 2015, p. 276

this matter.

Fourth, the dreamer herself believes these three dreams are precognitive, which reflects her awareness of a mysterious connection between her dreams and reality; otherwise, she wouldn't consider them precognitive.

So, is the woman's perception credible? This question is simple; it just needs to be verified.

The woman claimed that the first two treatments were not good and ended prematurely without results, and only the third one was the best, and the analyst this time was Jung. So, from the performance of these three dreams, can it be concluded that her dreams meet the requirements of the most basic laws of dreaming? The first two dreams were about her trying to cross the border but failing, which indicates that dreams and reality are indeed positively correlated. The second dream had light and fear, which means that the treatment process might be a bit tortuous, with both hope and frustration. The book does not explain this, but for the bad experiences in the dream, we can imagine what happened to her in reality: could it be that the analyst asked her to continue paying, but she felt that the treatment effect was not good? This is just a demonstration, and we don't know what exactly happened, but her description has shown that dreams and reality are positively correlated, and it is no problem that they conform to the most basic laws of dreaming. So, is the third dream really as effective as

Jung said? This also requires verification. Through analysis, this dream has the following correspondence with reality:

1) The first two dreams did not cross the border; only this dream did. Crossing the border can be seen as a breakthrough, a realization of a wish. Relatively speaking, this can be considered "evidence" of a better therapeutic effect, though whether the effect is short-term or long-term still needs discussion.

2) The dreamer claimed to find herself at a Swiss customs office, and Jung was Swiss. This further indicates that the woman's judgment was correct, and her dream was related to this therapy, as there was another link between the dream and reality— Switzerland. (It would be better if we knew the woman's nationality, but from the description, she shouldn't be Swiss; otherwise, she wouldn't say she crossed the border into Swiss customs.)

3) The dreamer only carried a handbag and thought she had nothing to declare. Unexpectedly, the customs officer pulled out two single beds from her handbag. In reality, Jung discussed marriage issues with her, and these two single beds can be seen as a symbol of her marital relationship. If this statement is true, it would mean that the woman's dream had actually predicted in advance what questions Jung, as the analyst, would ask her. However, since Jung was analyzing the psyche through dreams, rather than interpreting the dreams literally, he could not have discovered this point. He could only see information that was

helpful for his psychoanalysis—the single beds in the bag made him associate with sex, but he didn't realize there was another possibility, which was that he would definitely bring up this issue. Moreover, the customs officer also referred to Jung, who himself became a character in the dreamer's dream! This is very common. In the article "Can Scientific Experiments Prove Precognitive Dreams?" in the second volume, several dream examples show that the experiment organizers also appeared in the dreams of the subjects.

Regarding the correspondences, in addition to the three points mentioned above, plus the correspondence between the customs officer and Jung, there are actually four points of correspondence between this dream and reality. Consulting the content of "Specific Fulfillment" in the first volume, its fulfillment level belongs to "High-level Symbolic Dream Fulfillment." Unfortunately, it's not "High-level Direct Dream Fulfillment" or "High-level Direct Symbolic Fulfillment," which would have alerted Jung even more. As for Jung's belief that the therapeutic effect was very good, it can only be said that it was so compared to the other two analysts. If we disregard this point, the effect was actually far from as good as he thought, because the woman was not Swiss, and her border crossing was only a short-term act. To echo this, the therapeutic effect was likely also short-term. And from experience, the actual situation should also be short-term, because psychological illness is a mood; feeling good today and tomorrow doesn't mean feeling good the day after. A person's mood changes with the environment and is not immutable.

(2) Jung's Second Opportunity to Discover Precognitive Dreams

Like the dream mentioned above where Jung himself entered someone else's dream, there is another famous dream in the field of psychology about a "golden scarab." This dream was also made by a woman while undergoing psychoanalytic treatment with Jung. At the time, the treatment had reached a stalemate, and it was this dream that brought them a glimmer of hope, breaking the deadlock:

> Fourth Dream: I dreamed that someone gave me a scarab made of gold, a very precious piece of jewelry.

Just as the woman was describing her dream, something magical happened. A beetle resembling a scarab was hitting the window from outside, coinciding perfectly with the woman's words. Perhaps unintentionally, Jung opened the window, caught it, and handed it to the woman, saying: "Here! This is your scarab!" The woman was stunned by this scene, keenly realizing that this was exactly the scenario from her dream. This moved her deeply, and the pent-up emotions she had felt for days were instantly released, and she couldn't help but burst into tears. The treatment progressed from there.

This is actually a dream about therapy; the woman dreamed of what happened that very day while undergoing Jungian therapy, similar in principle to the third dream above. However, this dream contains elements of direct dreaming, making it easier to discern and allowing the dreamer to instantly understand what their dream is saying. The principle is a "déjà vu" effect triggered by the instantaneous "merging" of reality and the dream, causing the dreamer to have a sudden "epiphany." If you recall, there was also such a dream in Volume Two, about a landlord being scammed, which also occurred and was understood in real time. Below are the specific correspondences between this dream and reality, which also fully align with the most fundamental laws of dreams, conclusively demonstrating that this is a precognitive dream:

1) The dream featured someone gifting a scarab beetle; in reality, someone caught a scarab beetle and gave it to her.

2) The dream depicted the beetle as being made of gold, a very valuable piece of jewelry; in reality, an unexpected therapeutic outcome was achieved, precisely because the beetle's appearance helped the patient open up, pushing the therapy to a deeper level.

There are at least two corresponding points between this dream and reality: one is a direct-dreaming element, and the other is a symbolic-dreaming element. Classified by rank, it belongs to "Level 2 Direct-Symbolic Fulfillment." Clearly, this dream is easier to identify than the third one, yet Jung still did not consider it a precognitive dream. However, the fact that a scarab beetle appeared at that specific moment, neither sooner nor later, did arouse Jung's curiosity, because it was this very beetle that helped him break the deadlock and open up the patient's inner world. He believed this was by no means a random coincidence but rather revealed a profound connection between the human psyche and the world, constituting a paranormal phenomenon. Ultimately, he arrived at two explanations:

One represents "rebirth." He derived this meaning from the culture of ancient Egyptian primitive tribes, where the beetle symbolized "rebirth." When the woman saw this beetle, she successfully broke free from her inner predicament, which is precisely the artistic conception the beetle was meant to convey.

Another is the "synchronicity" effect. It refers to two or more events with no causal relationship occurring simultaneously, connected by some hidden link, making the coincidence meaningful. It includes three elements: no necessary causal relationship between events, temporal synchronicity of events, and the events having significance for the individual. Its value lies in providing people with some profound emotional connotation, creating emotional resonance.

Why Jung explained it this way is inseparable from his view of God. Jung often avoided the simple dichotomous question "Do you believe in God?", but he spent his life defending the psychological reality and value of religion and belief in God. This is very different from his mentor, Freud. In my humble opinion, from the perspective of psychological realism, Jung was a believer in God. Just as children of parents don't need to declare that they believe in their parents to be with them, because this blood relationship already transcends belief itself; it is a more stable, undeclared inner connection. This is somewhat similar to many people in our country who do not admit to believing in Buddhism but defend it, unconsciously reflecting the Buddhist worldview in their thoughts and actions.

(3) Jung's Third Opportunity to Discover Precognitive Dreams

When Jung was 48, the night before his mother passed away, he had this dream:

Fifth dream: As dusk fell, Jung walked alone through a dark forest. Under the shadows of ancient trees, jagged boulders lay scattered like the spines of monsters. In the dead silence, a sharp whistle suddenly pierced the air. Immediately after, a huge hound sprang from the bushes, its terrifying maw open, sweeping past like a dark shadow. Jung instantly understood: this hound was sent by the Wild Huntsman to claim someone's soul.

Jung awoke in a panic, receiving news of his mother's death that morning. Never had a dream shocked him so profoundly. Jung believed that a wild hunter out hunting with hounds at night symbolized the spirits of his Germanic ancestors calling for his mother. Why did Jung connect this dream with his mother? Besides the perfect timing, neither too early nor too late, there were at least two other correspondences between the dream and reality: first, the outcome matched, and second, the atmosphere matched. Undoubtedly, this was a precognitive dream, though not a "direct dream" as Jung defined it, but rather a "symbolic dream," symbolizing his mother's death.

The vast majority of precognitive dreams appear as "symbolic dreams," and 99% of dreams are like this, but Jung unfortunately didn't know. His core concept was "synchronicity," which is the acausal, meaningful coincidence of an inner psychological state with an external event in time. In his view, the root of this dream was not precognition, but a deep-seated concern for his mother's health hidden in his heart. This psychological archetype erupted in his subconscious on the night of his mother's death, coincidentally forming a "synchronistic" resonance with the actual death event.

As I've said in the second and third volumes, dreams related to the death of a loved one often have a strong impact on the living, causing emotional shock and leading people to believe in precognitive dreams. Jung, however, was an exception, because he was already lost in the trap he had set for himself. To pull him out, more such dreams would have to occur repeatedly, and to meet this condition, he would need more mothers, but how could that be possible? So, for him, it had already become a dead end.

(4) Jung's Fourth Opportunity to Discover Precognitive Dreams

The following three precognitive dreams were Jung's own, and they were likewise ignored by him:

1) In the autumn of 1913, Jung repeatedly dreamed of the European continent being submerged by floods, civilization being destroyed, and the sea turning blood red. In subsequent dreams, severe cold descended, and the land was covered with ice. The fact is, World War I broke out in 1914, and Europe plunged into bloody conflict.

2) There was once a young woman who sought treatment from Jung. Later, Jung dreamt that she jumped off a cliff to commit suicide, and he tried to stop her but failed. A few weeks later, the patient ended her life by taking an overdose of sleeping pills.

3) Before his death, Jung dreamt that he "ascended to a giant rock in the cosmos" and carved the important contents of his life onto the stone, feeling a sense of fulfillment upon completion.

The first was a dream foretelling World War I, which Jung

viewed as a reflection of a premonition of disaster within the collective unconscious; the second was a dream foretelling a patient's "suicide," which Jung saw as a warning from the subconscious regarding one's own psychological state; the third was a dream foretelling his own death, which Jung regarded as a symbol of the completion of life.

Symbolically speaking, Jung's interpretation was correct and aligned perfectly with "symbolic dreams," the most common type of precognitive dreams. However, Jung preferred to take a long detour, analyzing them through the psychological lens of his invented "subconscious and collective unconscious" rather than viewing them as precognitive. The reason for this was that among his many dreams, only a few appeared to be precognitive, making it impossible for him to draw a definitive conclusion. Yet, when he applied his own "formula" for interpretation, all of his dreams suddenly had answers. This result undoubtedly excited him, but it also caused the greatest secret to be buried. Little did he know that with just a bit more effort, he would have discovered even more precognitive dreams. Had he found more and then hypothesized that "most dreams are precognitive"—which is indeed the case (and inevitably so)—and then further hypothesized that "all dreams are precognitive," Jung would have found himself on the same path as the author.

## 3.2.2 Jung's Main Views on "Non-Precognitive Dreams"

Most precognitive dreams are symbolic dreams, but Jung's definition of precognitive dreams is rigidly fixed on the minority type of "direct dreams." So, when symbolic dreams—the "main force" of precognitive dreams—appear, his only option is to associate them solely with the patient's mental state, which is like "dropping the watermelon to pick up the sesame seeds." The "scarab beetle" dream is a good example; it was merely a precognitive dream. If the beetle in the dream had any meaning, it was on a very simple, real-world level. However, because he only associated it with the mental aspect, even when the truth was right in front of him, he couldn't see it. He could only choose the wrong answer, believing that "the beetle contained the patient's rebirth, of which the patient was unaware." —Jung himself was unaware, yet he claimed the patient was unaware; the patient's judgment was correct, yet in the end, the patient still had to pay Jung. Human society is just that strange. Of course, Jung could only analyze it this way; otherwise, how could dreams become a tool for psychoanalysis? If the patient's dream were acknowledged as precognitive, therapy could not proceed. Therefore, viewing all symbolic dreams with precognitive characteristics, and even all dreams, as "non-precognitive dreams" became a "wish fulfillment" for Jung and indeed for the entire field of psychology.

How did Jung misrepresent "non-precognitive dreams"? Below

are three of his representative views. These views are not outdated; they are still revered as the cornerstone of psychology, hindering people's breakthrough towards the only correct direction of precognitive dreams, thereby closing the door to dialogue with a broader knowledge system.

(1) Jung said: "Dreams often prepare, announce, and warn of certain situations long before they actually occur. This is not necessarily a miracle or clairvoyance. Most crises... have a long period of gestation[13]." Jung's mother's death was indeed not caused in a day; it truly underwent a long period of gestation. If we use this line of thinking to interpret those dreams mentioned in the article "Dreams of Final Moments" in the third volume—dreams of people who died from illness—it seems we can explain them as well. However, this interpretation is not foolproof, because although most crises do have long periods of gestation, this does not necessarily mean they will occur. Many crises also experience sudden reversals at the last moment, just as the "Dreams of Resurrection" in the third volume exemplify. Moreover, some dreams are not caused by death from illness but by sudden accidents. For such dreams, where is the period of gestation? This shows that the gaps in psychology do not fail to exist; rather, no one has exposed them.

---

[13] (UK) Anthony Stevens, *Private Dreams*, translated by Xue Xuan, Hainan Publishing House, 2015, p. 276

(2) Jung said: "It is wrong to call dreams that foretell the future prophetic dreams. Because they are no more prophetic than a medical diagnosis or a weather forecast. Such dreams are merely a combination of various possibilities created in advance, which may happen to coincide with events[14]." So it's not surprising that dreams that foretell the future come true. — It's true that symbolic dreams are no more prophetic than a medical diagnosis or a weather forecast. This is because symbolic dreams are "what you see is not what you get." On the surface, it's indeed difficult to know what they are saying. Medical diagnoses and weather forecasts, on the other hand, are straightforward; they say what they know, even if they are wrong. But in reality, symbolic dreams, like direct dreams, are equally infallible. We don't know this because we don't understand them, not because they truly lack this ability.

(3) Jung said: "The predictive ability of dreams does not mean that dreams can predict the future, but rather that dreams have a 'pre-cognition' of events that have not yet occurred. This is because the 'unconscious' can often perceive information that our consciousness cannot, and it reveals relevant information to people through dreams[15]." – Based on the laws of development, humans can indeed predict the next trend of things and achieve "pre-

---

[14] (UK) Anthony Stevens, *Private Dreams*, translated by Xue Xuan, Hainan Publishing House, 2015, p. 276

[15] Jung, C. G. *Man and His Symbols*. Translated by Zhang Juwen and Rong Wengu. Liaoning Education Press, 1988.

138

cognition." As for things without patterns, from Jung's explanation of "synchronicity" and "the unconscious," humans can still achieve this through dreams – although not scientifically verified, it still appeals to the general public, as the concept of "pre-cognition" does not contradict common sense. However, if the "unconscious" is believed to possess "supernatural" abilities, why can it only achieve "pre-cognition" and not "post-cognition"? In this regard, Jung's view lacks rigor. Of course, this is also due to the lack of his evidence – only a few dreams are precognitive, most are not – and this is the evidence of the entire field of psychology. But what they don't know is, isn't this incompleteness of evidence precisely what they themselves caused? If they had not actively dismissed the possibility that precognitive dreams are widespread, the situation would never have arisen.

In summary, psychology as represented by Jung not only distorted "non-precognitive dreams," but equally distorted "precognitive dreams," essentially constituting a holistic distortion of "dreams" themselves. Although he represented a major step forward compared to Freud, his authoritative position as a foundational figure merely shifted people's rigid thinking from one side to the other, allowing the truth to remain buried beneath the shackles of authority. How can this bondage be broken? The most thorough and only viable method is to propose the most radical hypothesis—"all dreams are precognitive"—and complete this seemingly impossible proof. If one merely advocates that "some dreams are precognitive," it will inevitably become endlessly entangled in endless disputes with "coincidence theory," "hallucination theory," "mysticism theory," and countless other such theories, making it impossible for the truth to ever see the light of day. Moreover, personal experience cannot be generalized to others; only by pursuing "all" can one construct an irrefutable, complete logical closed loop that leaves the other party speechless and ultimately ends this debate.

**Short-answer question:**

The perspective of precognitive dreams is clearly correct, yet is questioned as coincidence or superstition; the perspective of psychology is clearly wrong, yet is revered as science and truth. Please answer why this is the case from the perspective of transparency.

## 3.3 Christians' Misrepresentation of "Non-Precognitive Dreams"

It should be said that, Christians hold the most objective views on dreams among all people in the world. They acknowledge predictive dreams while refraining from making unfounded judgments about dreams. This cautious attitude is the reason why science has taken root in their community. However, every advantage comes with a disadvantage. This also makes it difficult for them to discover the secrets of dreams, because scientific discovery cannot be separated from in-depth research. If one merely treats dreams as something terrible to be avoided, it is equivalent to closing this door entirely. Nevertheless, the Bible is not actually as Christians understand it to be. Rather, Christians have misrepresented the true meaning of the Bible.

As the sole doctrine of Christianity, the Bible's evaluation of predictive dreams is the highest among all books in the world. The text records multiple predictive dreams from people of various social classes, including prisoners, common people, soldiers, ministers, pharaohs, and kings. The most notable point in the book is its prophecy that in the future, all people will have predictive dreams. For example:

the Book of Joel: "And afterward, I will pour out my Spirit on all people. Your sons and daughters will prophesy, your old men will dream dreams, your young men will see visions. Even on my servants, both men and women, I will pour out my Spirit in those days."

the Acts of the Apostles: "God said, In the last days, I will pour out my Spirit on all people. Your sons and daughters will prophesy, your young men will see visions, your old men will dream dreams. Even on my servants, both men and women, I will pour out my Spirit in those days, and they will prophesy."

The prophecies, visions, and unusual dreams mentioned therein primarily refer to precognitive dreams, because only precognitive dreams are something that every person can truly experience. It shocked me greatly to discover that such a book existed thousands of years ago with insights similar to this book. However, that statement is not entirely accurate, because since all dreams are precognitive, it actually means that the pouring out of God's Spirit upon people began from the moment humanity was born, and there is not a single day without it, rather than having to wait until "the latter days." Nevertheless, the flaw does not diminish the virtue—the Bible remains unmatched by any other book and is truly the pinnacle of human culture.

However, despite the Bible's high regard for predictive dreams, Christians influenced by this book exhibit a different behavior. From my interactions with Christians online, I discovered that they are only interested in dreams with obviously festive atmospheres and very certain predictive dreams, while they typically view nightmares as attacks from Satan and demons, the work of evil spirits, and are unwilling to discuss them further. That a Chinese person could change so dramatically simply by converting to Christianity left a deep impression on me at the time. One can only imagine what kind of behavior would be manifested among Westerners who have been steeped in Christianity since childhood.

如果催公真的信主了，那就放弃解梦吧！                         只看楼主    收藏    回复

新衣灯火

弟兄心

因解梦是不合圣经的教导。

"多梦和多言，其中多有虚幻，你只要敬畏神"。（传5：7）

"万军之耶和华说：不要被你们中间的先知和占卜的诱惑，也不要听信自己所做的梦，因为他们托我的名对你们说假预言，我并没有差遣他们。这是耶和华说的"（耶29：8-9）

"我已听见那些先知所说的，就是托我的名说的假预言，他们说：我做了梦，我做了梦。"……他们各人将所做的梦对邻舍述说，想要使我的百姓忘记我的名。"（耶23：25、27）

送TA礼物    ＋ 分享

举报 · 1楼  2010-06-29 22:40  回复

## Image 06

Fifteen years ago, I met a Chinese-American female netizen from the United States on Baidu Tieba. She was also a Christian, but was a rare "anti-Buddhism fighter" who frequently criticized Buddhism on Sina and Baidu Tieba, which drew my great attention. However, she was dismissive of my research on dreams and my interest in interpreting dreams for others, and even advised me to give up dream interpretation, saying it was contrary to biblical teachings. The screenshot(image 06) below shows her advice to me at that time; "Cui Gong Jiemeng" was my username back then. The content in the screenshot can be summarized in one sentence: "Do not believe in dreams, nor care what others say, only fear God." At that time, my understanding of the Bible was only superficial. I was greatly puzzled as to why the Bible said such things and could not understand why Christians were so cautious about dreams. The

Christian forum "God Loves Home" was very hostile to my interpreting dreams for others, and since I also questioned the Bible and criticized Christianity for being unscientific, I was frequently censored by them. Another Christian forum called "Jesus Loves You" went even further and directly stipulated in its rules a prohibition on dream interpretation: "Forbidden to post false testimonies about dreams, mysterious dreams, visions, or prophecies[16]."

Why did they hold such an attitude toward dream interpretation? It was only after I consulted the Bible that I discovered there were indeed such passages. However, I also found contradictions within it, because the Bible also contains accounts of Joseph and Daniel interpreting dreams for Pharaoh and kings. There are also such passages: "Do not interpretations belong to God?" and "Let the prophet who has a dream recount the dream, but let the one who has my word speak it faithfully (Jeremiah 23:28)." All of this shows that the Bible did not completely prohibit dream interpretation. Moreover, I found no support for what some Christians say about nightmares being from evil spirits or Satan the devil. Not only did I find no such support, but I actually found a passage that contradicts this. It was spoken by Job in the Book of Job: "So my bed will comfort me and my couch will ease the anguish of my complaint; even then you frighten me with dreams and terrify me

---

[16] https://tieba.baidu.com/p/6127782883

with visions (Job 7:13-14)." That is to say, in this passage, nightmares are also regarded as coming from God—God uses them to frighten humanity, not as tricks of Satan or demons. Only then did I understand that those Christians' views were merely their own interpretations; they were arbitrarily distorting the meaning, not what the Bible actually says. Moreover, there is another statement in the Book of Job that struck me as profound: "When deep sleep falls on people as they lie in their beds, God may speak in their ears and terrify them with warnings, to turn them from wrongdoing and keep them from pride (Job 33:15-16)." In other words: God created dreams, dreams created consciousness, and consciousness makes you remember lessons! And does this not align perfectly with what I say about "dreams being the source code of consciousness"? Now I cannot help but admire the Bible!

So why does the Bible say on one hand that dreams come from God, while on the other hand advising people not to believe in dreams? Isn't that contradictory? Upon further investigation, I discovered that it was related to the historical context at that time. The authors of these biblical passages were compelled by the pressures of their era to speak this way intentionally, for three main reasons: first, the need to strengthen faith; second, the need for national security; and third, the need to protect the people.

## 3.3.1 The need to strengthen faith

Bible Verse That Forbids Dream Interpretation #1:

(1) "If among you a prophet or a dreamer arises and gives you a sign or wonder, and the sign or wonder comes to pass, and he says, 'Let us go after other gods, which you have not known, and let us serve them,' you shall not listen to the words of that prophet or that dreamer." (Deut. 13:1–3)

(2) "That prophet or that dreamer, because he has taught rebellion against the LORD your God who brought you out of the land of Egypt and redeemed you from the house of slavery, to entice you away from the way that the LORD your God commanded you to walk— you shall certainly put him to death; so you shall purge the evil from your midst." (Deut. 13:5)

(3) "I have heard the prophets who prophesy lies in my name, saying, 'I had a dream, I had a dream.' They each tell their dreams to their neighbors to make my people forget my name, just as their ancestors forgot my name because of Baal." (Jer 23:25, 27)

(4) "As for those who use false dreams as prophecies and tell them, leading my people astray with lies and reckless words, I will oppose them. I did not send them or command them, and they bring no benefit to this people." (Jer 23:32)

The greatest difference between humans and animals is that humans have a sense of mystery; gazing up at the vast starry sky can create a synchronous resonance, allowing one to feel the mysterious power behind it. At that moment, the embryo of belief in God is unconsciously formed, so God must refer to that mysterious, unfathomable power behind the universe, and nothing else. But the problem is that not everyone will have this recognition, because what people understand best are concrete things verified by sight, not abstractions that require long contemplation to grasp. When someone interprets the mysterious force behind the universe in a concrete form, problems inevitably arise — in personifying it they also make it human-shaped. God is abstract and four-dimensional; an appropriate degree of personification is necessary, but turning God into a human form is different, because once God is made human-shaped, it effectively becomes three-dimensional and strays from the seed of faith. It is against this backdrop that the above scriptures appear. The Baal mentioned there refers to a human-shaped god; the Bible contains hundreds of passages admonishing people not to worship idols, and some of these relate to precognitive dreams. Since ancient people regarded dreams as possessing supernatural power, dreams carried unparalleled persuasive force and some inevitably exploited dreams. Thus, the Bible's opposition to dream interpretation is not actually directed at dreams themselves but at those who, under the banner of precognitive dreams, attempt to distort belief in God — a necessity for strengthening faith.

### 3.3.2 The Needs to National Security

Bible Verse That Forbids Dream Interpretation #2:

(5) "As for you, do not listen to your prophets, diviners, dream

interpreters, fortune-tellers, or sorcerers. These people unanimously tell you not to submit to the king of Babylon, but in fact they are deceiving you, so that you may be carried away captive, far from your homeland." (Jeremiah 27:9,10)

(6) "Thus says the Lord of hosts: 'Do not let your prophets and diviners who are among you deceive you, and do not listen to the dreams that you dream, for they prophesy falsely to you in My name. I have not sent them,' declares the Lord." (Jeremiah 29:8-9)

Since dreams can be exploited for religious purposes, they can certainly be exploited for political purposes as well. The dream of the Zhou king's campaign against the Shang dynasty, mentioned in the second volume, served exactly this role—it was this family's dream that solidified their determination to overthrow the Shang. However, this was because their dream was relatively straightforward and happened to be interpreted correctly. If it had been misrepresented, it could easily have backfired, leading to the destruction of the kingdom and family. The biblical passage above refers precisely to this point. At that time, the Kingdom of Judah was subordinate to the Neo-Babylonian Empire, but this subordination was humiliating in nature, somewhat similar to the relationship between the Song Dynasty and the Jin Dynasty in our history. At that time, the Song Dynasty emperor (the predecessor of Song Gaozong mentioned in the previous section) and numerous officials were taken captive to the Jin state as hostages.

A similar situation occurred in the Kingdom of Judah. Regarding how to deal with the Neo-Babylonian Empire in the future, Judah was also divided into two factions like the Song Dynasty: the war faction and the peace faction. Jeremiah, the author of this portion of biblical text, belonged to the peace faction. He advocated maintaining good relations with the Neo-Babylonian Empire rather than befriending Egypt. However, ultimately the war faction prevailed, choosing to ally with Egypt and antagonize Babylon. From the text, it appears that the banner raised by the war faction at the time was precognitive dreams; otherwise, Jeremiah would not have spoken this way.

History proved Jeremiah right. In 586 BCE, the Kingdom of Judah faced retaliation from King Nebuchadnezzar II of the Neo-Babylonian Empire, who personally led the military campaign. The Judahite king and his four sons were killed, and the Jewish people were almost entirely carried away as captives—an event known as the "Babylonian Captivity." Not until 539 BCE, when the Persian Empire under Cyrus II overthrew the Neo-Babylonian Kingdom, did these Jewish people end their humiliating captivity of nearly 50 years and return home. Judaism was born during this period, and its scriptures form the "Old Testament" portion of the Bible. The Old Testament is considered a flower blooming amid suffering, while the "New Testament" experienced even greater suffering due to Jesus's passion and the continuous persecution of Christianity.

Because of this, Christianity is more suited to those who have experienced profound suffering—and I am one such person. The cover of the Chinese edition of this series—published in 2025 and designed by the author—vividly illustrates this point: "A man being mercilessly swallowed by the sea is straining to hold a book above the water" (see postscript image 08). This image serves both as a poignant summary of his past years and as a prophetic foreshadowing of the trials this book series would face. More profoundly, it symbolizes how life's deepest spiritual awakening often arises from the anguish inflicted by the heaviest oppression. Thus, upon first encountering the Bible and Christianity, he was instantly captivated—deeply moved and profoundly shaken. Countless enlightening biblical texts—including Psalms and Proverbs from the Old Testament, and Romans and Ephesians from the New Testament—as well as Christianity's grand rituals connecting believers to the "Spirit," became the spiritual nourishment that drew him in wholeheartedly. He actively engaged in online Christian debates, voiced his thoughts in Bible-themed chat rooms, participated in church activities, browsed Christian-themed Baidu Tieba forums, and listened to Christian music—the central hypothesis of this book emerged precisely during that period. It was the Creator God, through a "controlled demolition" carried out by Christian civilization, who cleared his benighted mind, shattered his last vestige of stubbornness, and enabled him to achieve this unprecedented, epic breakthrough in human history. This breakthrough occurred in 2013, when he was not yet a member of Christianity. As time passed, in his assessment of major human cultural traditions, he gave Protestant Christianity a high score of 90—the highest rating among all cultures, topping the list (out of a possible 100). This result led him to re-examine the various flaws and shortcomings of Christianity, realizing that no culture in the world is perfect; only those that can still drive the continuous elevation of intellect and spirit amidst imperfection are worth following. Consequently, two years later, he resolutely joined Christianity and became a Christian. While the majority of people in the world began to distance themselves from Christianity because of its 10 points of flaws and shortcomings, he chose to draw near because of its high score of 90. This was not emotional—joining merely on the basis of fondness; it was rational—the result of weighing options, as the saying goes, "In hardship, choose the lesser evil; in prosperity, follow the greater good."

### 3.3.3 The need to protect the people

Bible Verse That Forbids Dream Interpretation #3:

(7) For when dreams increase and words grow many, there is vanity; but God is the one you must fear. (Ecclesiastes 5:7)

(8) "People consult idols and fortune-tellers, but the answers they get are nonsense. Some interpret dreams, but they only

deceive you; their comfort is useless. Therefore, people wander aimlessly, like lost sheep. They suffer because there is no shepherd to guide them." (Zechariah 10:2 GNT)

Although ancient people strongly believed in precognitive dreams, there were still many dreams that remained unexplained, especially nightmares. If dreams are considered positive and meaningful, how should nightmares be explained? While the Bible provides an affirmative answer regarding nightmares, the underlying reasoning remains unknown and incomprehensible. If they are attributed to Satan or demons, it seems more plausible, which is why the notion that nightmares come from Satan or demons has gained traction. This belief not only contradicts the Bible but also fosters superstition. So, how should such dreams be understood? Until the secrets of dreams are fully unveiled, the best approach is undoubtedly to ignore them. Hence, the Bible's discouragement of dream interpretation is, in fact, a form of protection for the people. Compared to those influenced by Buddhist or Taoist cultures, who might perform rituals or deliverances due to a nightmare, the biblical stance is far wiser.

In summary, Christianity's opposition to dream interpretation and its discouragement of believing in dreams is not a mistake, but rather a wise stance. This approach not only preserves the authority of precognitive dreams but also prevents people from being led astray by misrepresenting them. The reason Western society today still maintains a high degree of recognition and purity regarding precognitive dreams stems from the profound influence of the Bible. Likewise, the reason human society has reached its current level of scientific advancement is inseparable from the way the Bible's rigor shaped Western civilization. It can be said that without Christianity, which is rooted in the Bible, there would be no Western civilization today, and without Western civilization, there would be no Eastern civilization as it is today. Nearly all of humanity benefits from Christianity and the Bible, even those who oppose them; even those outside their direct sphere of influence are included. However, an advantage is not always an advantage. While Christianity's attitude toward dream interpretation has, to some extent, protected believers, it has also caused them to develop a resistance to dreams, making it difficult for them to uncover their mysteries. Even if someone makes a discovery, they are easily dismissed as a heretic. For this reason, when I informed more than ten "Chinese Christian publishers" in Hong Kong, Taiwan, Singapore, the United States, and other places of my intention to publish a book, not a single one responded, even after follow-up phone calls. I was willing to share the book's proceeds with them and even titled it "Evidence of the Creator's Existence" to attract their attention, but to no avail. Nevertheless, although Christianity does not encourage discussion of dreams, it is not forbidden. Such books can still be freely published in Western Christian countries, whereas in our own country, there is no such freedom, forcing this book to be published overseas. In this way, it has, in another form, benefited from Christianity! Why was science able to be born in Western Christian countries? Why do Christian countries account for the vast majority of Nobel Prizes? This gives a glimpse into the reasons.

Actually, it's not that banning the publication of superstitious books is entirely wrong; rather, when enacting a blanket prohibition, one must consider the existence of certain special cases to avoid treating what is not superstition as superstition and causing wrongful suppression. It is precisely because of the special nature of this book that people might not believe it, so the author has provided multiple ways of verification.To ban, without distinction, a sincere and responsible book like this is unreasonable. This not only reflects a slapdash work style in our cultural management, but also exposes shortcomings in our logical thinking and moral sense. Historically, there have been such lessons. From Copernicus, who discovered heliocentrism, to Wegener, who discovered continental drift, to Einstein, who proposed the photon hypothesis, nearly all proponents of revolutionary theories were initially branded as "heretics." This should have served as a warning to us, but we turned a blind eye. Perhaps we cannot entirely avoid this, but as a government shouldering the great mission of "governing the country and bringing peace to all," we should recognize that not only others make mistakes—we ourselves may make the same ones. The highest wisdom in governance should lie in ensuring the eradication of falsehoods while not strangling the faint voice that may represent the future.

**Short-answer question:**

In response to an approach that might cause the loss of benefits through a "one-size-fits-all" measure, Jesus gave a famous exhortation in the Bible. Which one is it?

# Postscript



## I. The Origin and Development of This Series and This Book

As many may not know, the *Unveiling Precognitive Dreams* series actually has a predecessor, which is the *Unveiling Dreams: All Dreams Are Precognitive Dreams* series (abbreviated as *Unveiling Dreams*). That series consists of four volumes, the first volume of which has been published in Simplified Chinese in Singapore (see image 08). The relationship between these two sets of books is simply that the titles, number of volumes, and size are different, while the content is basically the same.

Volumes 1, 2, and 3 of the *Unveiling Precognitive Dreams* series correspond respectively to Chapters 1, 2, and 3 of Volume 1 of the *Unveiling Dreams* series. The book you are reading now corresponds to Chapter 1 of Volume 2 of the latter. In other words: this series is actually formed by renaming and splitting another series.

Why split the original book? Why start with the fourth volume first? An introduction was originally made here, amounting to nearly five thousand words, but fearing it might cause difficulties for the platform, it had to be deleted. Therefore, it can only be replaced here with an ellipsis "..." to be introduced later when allowed or when there is an opportunity.

You might be concerned whether it would be a problem to skip the first three volumes and start reading directly from the fourth one? Certainly, starting from the first volume would be better, but it is not absolute; since each volume in this series presents an argument on the same proposition from a different perspective, it means that each volume is independent. Even if read out of order, the impact would not be significant, so there is no need to worry.

Image 08

## II. Introduction to the First Three Volumes of Unveiling Precognitive Dreams

### Volume I

*Unveiling Precognitive Dreams* Volume I, *Basic Theory of Dreams* (tentative title), is also Chapter 1 of its predecessor, *Unveiling Dreams: All Dreams Are Precognitive*. In the book, the author proposes new views on the characteristics, essence, classification, definition, functions, roles, and causes of dreams that are distinctly different from traditional cognition. In particular, the proposal of the concept of "dream perception(mengjue)" and the "fundamental law of precognitive dreams": the former asserts that dreaming is actually humanity's primary sensory perception system, while humanity's original primary sensory perception system is in fact the second. From this, it is deduced that consciousness originates from dreams, and that dreams are the "source code" of consciousness, thereby opening new avenues for understanding the brain's autonomous operating mechanisms. The latter points out that there exists a stable and unchanging law between dreams and the future; precognitive dreams are not unfathomable, but a phenomenon that everyone can understand. This provides theoretical support for people to discover more precognitive dreams and ensure their accuracy, and also serves as a verification guide for the verifiability and repeatability of this book series.

Given that there is a fundamental bias in human understanding of dreams, this book essentially reconstructs the theoretical system of dreams, transforming illusory dreams from unsolvable mysteries into a wondrous future science, laying a solid foundation for precognitive dream research to move towards empirical evidence and application.

## Volume II

*Unveiling Precognitive Dreams* Volume II, *The Arduous Journey of Discovering Precognitive Dreams* (tentative title), is also the second chapter of its predecessor, *Unveiling Dreams: All Dreams Are Precognitive*. The book answers a total of six questions:

First, why most ancients believed in precognitive dreams

Second, the current status of precognitive dreams in the contemporary Chinese dream interpretation community

Third, can scientific experiments prove precognitive dreams?

Fourth, how long does it take to have the same type of precognitive dream as others?

Fifth, why don't you believe in precognitive dreams?

Sixth, why do I believe in precognitive dreams

The first two points focus on history and the current state of affairs; the most important are the last four points: the third point explains whether scientific experiments can actually prove precognitive dreams, and why experiments already conducted in laboratories have failed to prove them; the fourth and fifth points explain why, among people, some believe in precognitive dreams while others do not; the sixth point introduces the author's arduous process of cracking precognitive dreams, including experiences unknown to the public during that period. I believe the answers to these questions will surely provide readers with meaningful inspiration. Whether you believe or not right now, these answers are worth looking forward to—because for you, the time for them to take effect is not now, but in the future; if you can attach importance to them now, you will be able to seize the opportunity and stand firm at the forefront when the time comes.

## Volume III

*Unveiling Precognitive Dreams* Volume III, Public Manifestations of *All Dreams are Precognitive* (tentative title), also serves as the third chapter of its predecessor, *Unveiling Dreams: All Dreams are Precognitive*. This book aims to find empirical support for the hypothesis that "all dreams are precognitive." The logic is as follows: if this hypothesis holds true, there must exist certain "public manifestations" that can be directly or indirectly observed by humans. For example, the public manifestation of the Earth's rotation is the Big Dipper revolving around the North Star every night; the public manifestation of light's wave nature is the formation of alternating light and dark fringes on a screen when light passes through double slits; and the public manifestation of electromagnetic induction is the generation of an electric current when a magnet moves through a coil. Precognitive dreams should be no different; it is simply that no one has discovered them until now. As it turns out, just as hypothesized, the author has not only found such manifestations but has also discovered two unique types of precognitive dreams: "Exo-coupled Chiral Dreams" and "Endo-coupled Chiral Dreams."

A "Chiral Dream" is a type of mirror image. Its most significant characteristic is its ability to "respond to all changes with constancy"—maintaining the mirror image even amidst dynamic shifts, which in itself represents a law. Since it is a law, it effectively pushes human research into precognitive dreams onto an "unquestionable" royal road—leaving opponents with no choice but to gaze at the ocean and sigh in futility should they wish to object further.

## III. Introduction to "Unveiling Precognitive Dreams" Volume 5

*Unveiling Precognitive Dreams* Volume 5, fully titled *Unveiling Precognitive Dreams: The Distortion of Dreams by Culture-Bound Syndromes*, will be published within three months barring exceptional circumstances. This volume is essentially a continuation of the fourth, but approaches the subject from the perspective of traditional culture, taking common misconceptions in Traditional Chinese Medicine and Buddhism as entry points:

1. Addressing the TCM view that "excessive dreaming" and

"frequent nightmares" are pathological conditions requiring intervention through medication and medical treatment, this book proposes a diametrically opposite viewpoint: these two phenomena not only require no treatment but are actually highly beneficial to the body—especially nightmares, which, besides being precognitive dreams, play a crucial role in helping the human body avoid sudden death under high stress.

2. Addressing the Buddhist attribution of nightmares to "harassment by demons" and the interpretation of deceased persons appearing in dreams as "posthumous dream communication," thereby advocating resolution through rituals and ceremonies to deliver the spirits, this book solemnly points out: such thoughts and practices not only easily lead individuals into the quagmire of superstition but also cause immense harm to the development of society as a whole. In reality, both types of dreams are also precognitive dreams and rehearsals for individual survival, contrary to Buddhist claims.

Unless the above facts are clarified, the truth cannot be revealed. This book places them under the spotlight of reason and science for the first time, fundamentally uprooting the soil in which superstition thrives—this step alone holds significance far beyond the ordinary. However, despite this, the author remain somewhat apprehensive about the publication of this book, because scientific discoveries are inseparable from criticism and correction, a process that inevitably disrupts the existing order and triggers controversy, making it difficult for this book to pass review. After all, up to now, this is merely my one-sided account and has not yet gained social recognition. Yet to gain social recognition, the book must first be published; and to get the book published, it must first pass social recognition—this is clearly a "paradox"! Since the likelihood of this book passing review is very small, publication may be temporarily postponed in favor of publishing the sixth volume first. The subtitle of the sixth volume has not yet been finalized; it could be *All "Dreams of the Dead" Are Precognitive Dreams*, or it could be The *Role Played by the Deceased in Dreams*, with the final result to be determined.

Finally, please help promote this book. The more people know about this book, the more motivated the author will be to bring the subsequent volumes to you as soon as possible; otherwise, he will likely first translate the books currently being published into multiple languages (such as German, French, Spanish, Portuguese, Italian, Japanese, Dutch, etc.) before he can attend to the subsequent volumes. This is because the earliest purchasers of this book are generally people who believe in precognitive dreams, and such readers are evenly distributed globally. This means that to achieve significant popularity and sales for this book, the coverage must be expanded—by first translating the books currently being published into multiple languages, and once this is done, for you who have already purchased this book, it will undoubtedly be an anxious wait.

## IV. About the author

Author of this book, English pen name: S.F. Heaven; full English name: Sole Fool Under Heaven. Real Chinese name: Cui Yi; childhood and adolescent name: Gong Li; Chinese pen name in pinyin: Tian Shang Tian Xia Wei Wo Du Chun. Independent researcher. Began studying dreams in midlife; after nearly two decades of dedicated effort, single-handedly solved the age-old mystery of dreaming, proving the seemingly impossible proposition that "all dreams are precognitive."

Anyone encountering this name for the first time inevitably wonders: Why such self-deprecation? Yet, who doesn't wish to be praised? Who would willingly invite criticism? The author is no exception—he too cherishes praise and recoils from censure. Yet he adopted this name not out of self-contempt or self-abasement, but rather as a deliberate act of personal exemplification—both for himself and for his readers:

First, he deeply values critique. Praise brings comfort; criticism jolts us awake. By deliberately choosing to bear the latter, he seeks to break free from his own habitual patterns—turning the edge of scrutiny inward, toward himself first.

Second, he observes a prevailing social tendency: everyone

craves compliments, and dissenting or unwelcome opinions are widely avoided. This pervasive "craving for praise" subtly constrains the freedom of expression. Rather than waiting for the environment to change, he begins with himself: by criticizing himself first, he clears the way to speak truthfully.

Third, he has witnessed the degradation of the term "public intellectual"—a label that was originally meant to denote a certain identity but has now devolved into a defensive shield: whoever slaps it onto someone else gains temporary safety. When no one is willing to claim a word anymore, genuine discussion has already ended, leaving only a prisoner's dilemma of mutual labeling. He refuses to play this game—but neither can he pretend it doesn't exist. So he places himself squarely on stage, beginning by criticizing himself, thereby cracking open a fissure in this stalemate.

Fourth, his research repeatedly ventures into the "unspeakable." While dreams point toward the future, they inevitably point toward taboos—those cognitions enshrined as axioms by tradition, those interventions taken for granted by custom. Once placed under the spotlight of reason and science, they cannot help but reveal their underlying falsehoods and superstitions. Yet clarification means offense, and correction means disruption. When a manuscript that exposes truth must seek publishing opportunities through deletions and delays, the author feels more acutely than ever the difficulty of content compliance, and thus resolves all the more firmly: to break self-sealing with self-mockery, and to earn self-honesty through self-condemnation.

Fifth, dreams are each person's most intimate inner dialogue, custom-tailored to every individual, and closely related to personal privacy. To unveil the secrets of dreams inevitably requires the exposure of personal privacy. Therefore, more detailed information about the author is provided in the book, and I shall not elaborate further here.

## V. Other Issues

### (I) Regarding Post-Lesson Test Questions

Each topic in this book concludes with a set of test questions, including short answers, multiple choice, true/false, and fill-in-the-blanks. These questions are designed to help readers consolidate their understanding and self-assess their mastery of the material. At the same time, they serve to inspire those who seek to challenge the book, helping them reflect more deeply on their own perceptions rather than jumping to conclusions.

Answers to most of the test questions can be found within the book; only a very small portion requires personal insight or external knowledge. If you find yourself confused even while referring to the text, it indicates that you have not yet truly grasped the essence of the book and require further study. Standard answers will not be included with the book; please pay attention to the author's announcements for details.

(II) Regarding the Translation of This Book

The translation of this book was completed using translation software, errors are unavoidable, if you have any questions, please verify with the author via the book's official website or relevant social media; you may also consult someone around you who understands Chinese to check if there are translation errors. The author sincerely thanks every reader who has raised questions or offered suggestions.

(III) Regarding the Official Website for This Book

The official website identifier for this book is: "yzmjm," the acronym formed from the initial letters of the Chinese pinyin "Yu Zhi Meng Jie Mi." Domain registration has just been completed, and the site will go live once the book achieves sufficient sales volume. The international official website and domestic official website domains are respectively: yzmjm.com and yzmjm.cn. Temporarily unable to access.

This site welcomes readers, scholars, and researchers interested in topics related to precognitive dreams to explore this new cognition with the author here, based on respect for facts and reason. It also welcomes visionary academic institutions, technology enterprises, and investment partners with a strategic vision to participate with the author in the early construction of this pioneering cognitive ecosystem.

## (IV) Warning

Finally, a reminder to everyone:

Do not illegally reproduce this book!

Do not steal the profits from this book!

Do not restrict freedom of speech!

Do not interfere with the distribution and sale of this book!

Do not use AI to rewrite this book for profit!

Do not purchase pirated e-books or physical books!

Please do not be a "freeloader"—only riding along without intending to give anything in return! Even if you have no intention of respecting the author's labor, you should at least respect your own dreams. Your dream stands far above you; it witnesses everything and records everything, serving as the sacred bridge between you and the great Dreamweaver. May you hold a book in your hands as if holding your own dream; may you revere the book in your heart as if revering divine revelation. If we live by the Spirit, by the Spirit let us also walk!